A Bibliography
of the Writings of
Walter H. Pater

Garland Reference Library of the Humanities (Vol. 6)

A Bibliography
of the Writings of
Walter H. Pater

Samuel Wright

Garland Publishing, Inc., New York & London

1975

Copyright © 1975

by Garland Publishing, Inc.

All Rights Reserved

Library of Congress Cataloging in Publication Data

Wright, Samuel, 1905-
    A bibliography of the writings of Walter H. Pater.

    1. Pater, Walter Horatio, 1839-1894--Bibliography.
I. Title.
Z8664.W75   016.824'8   74-30448
ISBN 0-8240-1062-0

Printed in the United States of America

In Memoriam

KEITH WRIGHT
1937-1973
Poet

"Poetry is intensity"

Contents

List of Illustrations

Preface

The first section commences with a chronological record or list (I a.) of all Walter Pater's published writings, in order that the reader can study the growth of his style and ideas. It is hoped that it will also be useful for purposes of reference. Books are only mentioned briefly in this Record as full descriptions are given in the next sub-section (I b.)

I have dealt with the first English and American editions up to the date of the New Library Edition, 1910, and with any later uncollected publications which might have first edition interest.

The dates given for most of the reprints of the books are those when the printing was ordered, whereas the first and other editions bear the dates of actual publications.

Acknowledgements

The help I have received in compiling this bibliography during the last twelve years has been on such a generous scale that I would like to record my thanks to those people and libraries who have helped me. I hope that I shall not have omitted too many names in what follows.

First, I would like to salute those people whom I discovered as having met and spoken to Walter Pater. They were able to describe him to me and give me their memories of his humour and unfailing kindness.

Pride of place now comes to the present custodian of the Pater copyright, who entertained me and has allowed me to print a poem by Pater and refer to various unpublished letters.

Mr. John Sparrow, Warden of All Souls College, Oxford,

doyen of Pater scholars and collectors, has been helpful to me from the beginning and freely allowed me to examine his fascinating collection of books, manuscripts and letters.

Professor Ian Fletcher, Reading University, has placed me deeply in his debt with regard to Pater's library borrowing, a debt not yet paid.

Over the last ten years I have received much help from scholars in Australia, Africa, South America, Canada, Japan, and, most of all, U.S.A. either by correspondence or when I have met them on their pilgrimages to Britain. They are too many to mention, but I would like to record my gratitude to Dr. Laurence G. Evans, Harvard and Northwestern Universities, who has been of immense assistance to me in so many ways. The Clarenden Press, Oxford, have given me permission to refer to Dr. Evan's invaluable *Letters of Walter Pater* (1970) for which I use the abbreviation *LWP*.

I would also like to thank Dr. Robert Seiler of Liverpool University for the opportunity to read and use the draft of his forthcoming book on Pater in the Critical Heritage Series.

The Curator of Manuscripts, The Houghton Library, Harvard University, has allowed me to publish the Accessions Record of their Pater manuscripts.

The Librarian of Winchester College, Mr. J.M.G. Blakiston, has enlightened me on the scope of the Blakeney Press and given me much interesting biographical information on its founder.

Mr. Benton L. Hatch, Massachusetts, furnished me with much valuable information on Thomas Bird Mosher and his publications.

The Rev. L.M. Styler, Brasenose College, was extremely helpful to me in the early days of my work and from him I obtained the copy of the funeral oration on Pater which is printed in an appendix.

The Macmillan Press Limited have kindly allowed me to quote from their agreement with Walter Pater for the publication of *STUDIES IN THE HISTORY OF THE RENAISSANCE* (1873) and provided me with much interesting data on dates and numbers of publications. The Majority of my notes were made at the British Museum Library, a Titan but not weary. The Bodleian Libraries, old, new and very old, have been a great source of help to me by reason of the diversity of their resources and character. The University of London Library has afforded material not available elsewhere and I would like to thank Mrs. Joan Gibbs for so much unsolicited help. I would also like to register my thanks to the staffs of the universities of Lancaster, Cambridge and Essex.

This brings me to the very generous assistance I have received from three Oxford Colleges: Worcester, where I gained much helpful information on the Daniel Press; Brasenose, where Mr. Robin Peedel has been kind beyond measure on many occasions; and Queens, where I found scarce books and the register of Pater's borrowings in his early Oxford days.

I have been helped at many smaller local libraries, and I think here of Torquay; Penzance; the Harris Library, Preston; and most of all my local library of the Borough of Colchester, where over the years I have been the recipient of so much kindness from so many members of the staff.

SECTION I   PUBLISHED WRITINGS

a. CHRONOLOGICAL RECORD of all Periodical and
        Book Publications

    Order of listing:

        1. Chronological order of composition, if known

        2. If date of composition is not known, or cannot
            be deduced, then the order of publication
            is given

        3. When no exact date is known:

                a. Periodical items are placed as at
                    the end of the month

                b. Books are dated as at the end of the
                    year of publication

    UPPER CASE TITLES refer to books by Pater.

CONTENTS of the RECORD (in Chronological Order)

No.	Date	Title
84	10 Aug. 1892	MARIUS THE EPICUREAN: HIS SENSATIONS AND IDEAS (Third edition)
85	9 Sept. 1892	Introduction to The Purgatory of Dante Alighieri (Purgatorio I - XXVII) (Translated by Charles Lancelot Shadwell)
86	Oct. 1892	Raphael
87	9 Feb. 1893	PLATO AND PLATONISM: A SERIES OF LECTURES
88	10 June 1893	Mr. George Moore as an Art Critic [Review]
89	7 Nov. 1893	The Age of Athletic Prizemen: A Chapter in Greek Art
90	Nov. 1893	Apollo in Picardy
91	Dec. 1893	THE RENAISSANCE: STUDIES IN ART AND POETRY (Fourth edition)
92	Jan. 1894	Some Great Churches in France 1. Notre-Dame d'Amiens
93	Mar. 1894	Mr. F.W. Bussell
94	May 1894	Some Great Churches in France 2. Vézelay
95	June 1894	AN IMAGINARY PORTRAIT [The Daniel Press]

POSTHUMOUS PUBLICATIONS

No.	Date	Title
96	July 1894	Pascal
97	11 Jan. 1895	GREEK STUDIES: A SERIES OF ESSAYS
98	11 Oct. 1895	MISCELLANEOUS STUDIES: A SERIES OF ESSAYS
99	6 Oct. 1896	GASTON DE LATOUR: AN UNFINISHED ROMANCE
100	1896	ESSAYS FROM THE 'GUARDIAN'
101	1903	UNCOLLECTED ESSAYS BY WALTER PATER
102	1910	COLERIDGE'S WRITINGS
103	1919	SKETCHES AND REVIEWS
	1 Apl. 1931	Imaginary Portraits: 2. An English Poet (See No. 29)

CONTENTS of the RECORD (in Alphabetical Order)

xix

Title	Year	No.
"The Complete Poetical Works of Wordsworth . . . " [Review] (<u>Athenaeum</u>)	1889	61
"The Complete Poetical Works of Wordsworth . . . " [Review] (<u>Guardian</u>)	1889	62

1   THE CHANT OF THE CELESTIAL SAILORS   (written) Spring 1856
    Poem

    ─────────────

    Printed and published by Edward Henry Blakeney at his
    Private Press, Winchester, (March) 1928.   30 copies only.
    For a full description and comment, together with a note on
    the Blakeney Press, see Section Ib, Books, No. 13

    ─────────────

    This poem was written in the Spring of 1856 while Pater was a
    scholar at King's School, Canterbury.

    It should not be confused with the 'lost' poem: "Chant of the
    Celestial Sailors when they first put out to Sea."
    For the latter, see Section IIa, The 'lost' writings, No. 1

    For an account of the poetry written by Pater which has survived
    see Section IIc, Poetry

2   INSCRIPTION FOR THE LIFE OF WALTER PATER   (written) March 1859
    Poem

    ─────────────

    Printed and published by Edward Henry Blakeney at his Private
    Press, Winchester 1928.   14 copies only.
    For a full description and comment, with opinion as to the
    authenticity of this poem, together with a note on the
    Blakeney Press, see Section IIb, Books, No. 14

3   Diaphaneite   (written) July 1864

    ─────────────

    First published in:
    MISCELLANEOUS STUDIES (1895), pp. 251-259
    See Section Ib, Books, No. 8

    ─────────────

MISCELLANEOUS STUDIES was a posthumously published book prepared
for the press by Pater's friend, Charles Lancelot Shadwell.   He
explained in the Preface to that book why he came to publish this
essay, and stated: "It is with some hesitation that the paper on
Diaphaneite, the last in this volume, has been added, as the only
known specimen to be preserved of those early essays of Mr.
Pater's, by which his literary gifts were first made known to the
small circle of his Oxford friends."

The small circle was probably the Old Mortality, a society

founded by a student of Balliol, John Nicholl, in November 1856,
and it is thought that this essay was read before the society.
Pater joined the Society at the end of 1862 or early in 1863.
The weekly meetings did not last after 1866 although reunions
were held until 1876. The Society had many distinguished
members, including G.B. Hill, A.C. Swinburne, T.H. Green, A.E.
Mackay, H. Nettleship, E. Caird and J.A. Symonds. It was
instituted for the reading of essays and for vigorous and high
spirited debate, "the free discussion of everything in heaven or
earth." In art, literature, politics and religion, the Society
was avowedly "radical." (see Gerald C. Monsman, "Old Mortality
at Oxford," Studies in Philology, LXVII, 3 July 1970

The manuscript of this essay is at King's School, Canterbury.

4   Coleridge's writings   (written) 1865
    [unsigned review]

    Conversations, Letters and Recollections of S.T. Coleridge,
    edited by Thomas Allsop, (London) T. Farrah, 1864

    _____

    Westminster Review
    No. LVII, Vol. LXXXV o.s., XXIX n.s. (January 1866), ART IV,
    106-132

    Part of this essay, extensively revised and with many and
    lengthy omissions, was joined to a revised version of Pater's
    Introduction to the selection of poems by "Samuel Taylor
    Coleridge" published in The English Poets (1880-1883), see
    No. 32, to appear in:

    APPRECIATIONS (1889), pp. 64-106
    as "Coleridge". (see No. 71)

    COLERIDGE'S WRITINGS was published as a small 3½" x 5¾" book
    by Gowans & Gray, London and Glasgow (1910) as No. 40 of
    Gowan's International Library. An introductory note stated:
    "As none of Walter Pater's works have been reprinted in this
    country in a really cheap form, it is hoped that the present
    booklet will be appreciated by many. The essay it contains
    was first published in the Westminster Review for January
    1866, and afterwards reprinted in the volume called
    APPRECIATIONS." This was a paper backed book of 48 pages,
    priced 6d. (see No. 102)

    Part of this essay, taken from those portions which did not
    appear in APPRECIATIONS, appeared in book form in:
    SKETCHES AND REVIEWS, edited by Albert Mordell, published by
    Boni and Liveright (New York) 1919, as "Coleridge the
    Theologian". (see No. 103)

    "Coleridge's Writings" thus appears in three versions: Nos. 4
    71 and 103, with the verbatim reprint published by Gowan and
    Gray No. 102. The three versions are collated in Appendix

---

In a letter to William Sharp, dated Nov. 4, 1882, Pater speaks of
"an article on Coleridge in the Westminster of January 1866, with
much of which, both as to matter and manner, I should now be
greatly dissatisfied.   That article is concerned with S.T.C.'s
prose, but, corrected, might be put alongside of the criticism of
his verse which I made for Ward's "English Poets."   The letter
can be read in William Sharp: a Memoir by Elizabeth Sharp
(Heinemann) 1910, pp. 67-68, or in LWP No. 69.

5   Winckelmann   (written) 1866
       [unsigned review]

       The History of Ancient Art among the Greeks by John
       Winckelmann, translated from the German by G.F. Lodge
       8vo. London: 1850

       Biographifische Aufsatze von Otto Jahn. Leipzig. 1866

       Westminster Review
       No. LXI, Vol. LXXXVII, o.s., XXXI n.s. (Jan. 1867), ART IV,
       pp. 80-110

       First printed in book form in:
       STUDIES IN THE HISTORY OF THE RENAISSANCE (1873), 146-206

       A separate edition of Winckelmann was published by Gowans
       and Gray, 59 Cadogan Street, Glasgow, in May 1912, 18mo.
       swd, 6d.

In a letter dated 12 Nov. 1866 to Dr. John Chapman, editor of the
Westminster Review , Pater wrote: "I shall be glad to have my
article inserted in the January No.   There are however a good
many minute corrections which I should like to make in it, and
I shall therefore be glad, if it is not giving you too much trouble
if you will return the MS for that purpose, and also let me know
on what date it will be necessary to forward it to you for press."
LWP. No. 7

6   Poems by William Morris   (written by 23rd June 1868)
       [unsigned review]

       The Defence of Guenevere and other Poems
           by William Morris 1858

The Life and Death of Jason: a Poem
    by William Morris 1867

The Earthly Paradise: a Poem
    by William Morris 1868

Westminster Review
No. LXVIII, Vol. XC o.s., XXXIV n.s. (Oct. 1868), Art II
pp. 300-312

Part of this review, pp. 300-309, with some revisions, was
reprinted in:
APPRECIATIONS (1889), pp. 213-227, as "Aesthetic Poetry",
but omitted from the second and later editions of that book.

It is interesting to compare the periodical (1868) review
with the version which appeared in APPRECIATIONS (1889) and
a note on this will be found in Appendix b 1.

Thomas Bird Mosher (Portland, Maine, U.S.A.) published
"Aesthetic Poetry" under the heading "Two Appreciations: I.
Aesthetic Poetry II. Dante Gabriel Rossetti" in The Bibelot
V (Oct. 1899, 303-319. I quote the following from
Mosher's own introduction to this item: "One must read
Aesthetic Poetry to realise just what was the unique graft
upon English Literature conferred by William Morris. It is
the most subtily interpretative of all judgements upon his
poetry, not even excepting Swinburne's magnificent meed of
praise. As a prose introduction to the cycle of the
Earthly Paradise it cannot be surpassed. And this method
when applied to eliciting Rossetti's supreme gifts is fully
essential to our appreciation of him."

"Aesthetic Poetry" was reprinted in:
SKETCHES AND REVIEWS (1919), edited by Albert Mordell,
published by Boni and Liveright (New York). (See No. 103)
This book purported to collect Pater essays not hitherto
published in book form. Mr. Mordell informed me that he
included "Aesthetic Poetry" because it had been removed
from the second and subsequent editions of APPRECIATIONS.

A letter from Miss Hester M. Pater, Pater's elder sister, to
Charles L. Shadwell, headed 6 Canning Place, May 12 (n.y.)
stated: "We wrote to ask Mr. Macmillan if he had any
objection to Mr. Daniel printing "Aesthetic Poetry". He had
no objection - so will you kindly tell Mr. Daniel that we
shall be very pleased for him to print it in his charming
style . . . " Nothing came of this proposal.

The remainder of this review, pp. 309-412, was reprinted in:
STUDIES IN THE HISTORY OF THE RENAISSANCE (1873), pp. 207-213
(see No. 16) as "Conclusion"; was omitted from the second
edition (1877); but restored by Pater in the third edition

4

(1868) and the fourth edition (1893).
Thus four versions of this piece appeared in Pater's lifetime
the Westminster Review review as above and those in the 1st,
3rd and 4th editions of THE RENAISSANCE. In Appendix b 2
will be found a survey of the differences, not only of
punctuation and minor expression, but of significant thought
between the four printings.

Thomas Bird Mosher (Portland, Maine, U.S.A.) published an
extract from this review ("Well, we are all condamnes, as
Victor Hugo says . . . and simply for those moments sake") in
The Bibelot, III (Sept. 1897), [285]

7   Notes on Leonardo da Vinci   1 November 1869

The Fortnightly Review
No. XXV, Vol. XII o.s., VI n.s. (1 November 1869), 494-508

First printed in book form in:
STUDIES IN THE HISTORY OF THE RENAISSANCE (1873), pp. 90-122
as "Lionardo da Vinci" (see No. 16)

This essay was published by Thomas Bird Mosher (Portland,
Maine, U.S.A.) in The Bibelot, VI (February 1900), pp. 37 -
[76]. Mosher supplied an introduction. He included the
medallion portrait, a sonnet: "For our Lady of the Rocks" by
Dante Gabriel Rossetti, and an extract from J.A. Symonds's
Renaissance in Italy, Vol. II, 312-327

8   A Fragment on Sandro Botticelli   1 August 1870

The Fortnightly Review
No. XLIV, Vol. XIV o.s., VIII n.s. (1 August 1870), pp. 155-160

First printed in book form in:
STUDIES IN THE HISTORY OF THE RENAISSANCE (1873), pp. 39-51
as "Sandro Botticelli". (see No. 16)

This essay was published by Thomas Bird Mosher (Portland,
Maine, U.S.A.) in The Bibelot, Vol. III (September 1897), pp.
287 - [314] as "Sandro Botticelli, Luca della Robbia, Two
Renaissance Studies by Walter Pater". Mosher supplied an
appreciative introduction, and included short extracts from
the "Conclusion" and the "Preface" of THE RENAISSANCE

The Fortnightly Review
No. LVIII, Vol. XVI o.s., X n.s. (1 October 1871), pp. 377-386

First printed in book form in:
STUDIES IN THE HISTORY OF THE RENAISSANCE (1873), pp. 18-38
(see No. 16)

The works of Pico della Mirandula, 1463-1494, were edited and
published in 1496 by his nephew, Giovanni Pico, at Bologna, the
Life being included as an Introduction.

The English translation by Sir Thomas More was published in 1510 by
John Rastell (More's brother-in-law), though it had been written
in 1504/5: The Life of John Picus Erle of Mirandula, a Great
Lorde of Italy, an excellent connying man in all sciences and
Vertuous of Living . . . Translated out of Latin into Englische
by Maister Thomas More.

A facsimile of William Rastell's (More's nephew) edition of 1557
can be studies in The English Works of Sir Thomas More, 7 vols.,
with an introduction and philological notes by A.W. Reed (Eyre and
Spottiswoode 1921) - a triumph of high scholarship. Professor
Reed drew attention to the appeal of More's style to Pater, and
noted an odd blunder in Pater's adaptation of More's description
of the young humanist (p. 26). "He was of feature and shape seemly
and beateous of stature, goodly and high of flesh and soft, his
visage lovely and fair, his colour white intermingled with comely
rede, his eyes grey and quick of look, his teeth white and even,
his hair yellow and abundant and trimmed with more than the usual
artifice of his time". Reed says: "the words in Italics are
Pater's, More's rendering being: "his hair yellow and not too
picked". Thus Pater's version is rather opposite in meaning to
the original.

The Brasenose College Library register of books borrowed records
the following 3 volumes taken out by Pater

        Pico Miranduloe Opera   Sept. 1870
        Sir Thomas More's Works   Jan. - Feb. 1871
        Picus of Mirandula Works   Jan. - Mar. 1871

10 The Poetry of Michelangelo   1 November 1871

The Fortnightly Review
No. LIX, Vol. XVI o.s., X n.s. (1 November 1871), 559-570

First printed in book form in:
STUDIES IN THE HISTORY OF THE RENAISSANCE (1873), pp. 62-89.
(see No. 16)

This essay was published by Thomas Bird Mosher (Portland,
Maine, U.S.A.) in The Bibelot, Vol. IV (April 1898), 127 -
[157], as "The Poetry of Michelangelo by Walter Pater."
Mosher supplied a short introduction, and included a sonnet
by Giordano Bruno (?) (trans. J.A. Symonds), and a short
quotation from Symonds's History of the Italian Renaissance.

11 "Children in Italian and English Design"   15 July 1872
    by Sidney Colvin
    with illustrations
    (Seeley, Jackson and Co.)

The Academy
No. 52, Vol. III (July 15, 1872), pp. 267-268

This little known review has not been reprinted in any form, and
is not mentioned in any list or bibliography.

In Section I b BOOKS, will be found a list of those known writings
by Walter Pater which do not appear in either the Edition de Luxe
of 1900/1901 or the New Library Edition 1910.

In view of the choice of Pater as the reviewer of this book, it is
interesting to note that a number of reviews of his first book
THE RENAISSANCE (1873) were placed in the Art columns of the
periodicals in which they appeared, and Pater himself spoke of it
as a work of art.

12 Aucassin and Nicolette   (written) 1872

First printed in:
STUDIES IN THE HISTORY OF THE RENAISSANCE (1873) pp. 1-17
(see No. 16)

In the second and subsequent editions this was revised and
included with an account of a thirteenth century story: "Li
Amitiez de Ami et Amile" under the title: "Two Early French
Stories"

13 Luca della Robbia   (written) 1872

First printed in:
STUDIES IN THE HISTORY OF THE RENAISSANCE (1873) pp. 53-61
(see No. 16)

This essay was published by Thomas Bird Mosher (Portland, Maine
U.S.A.) in The Bibelot, Vol. III (September 1897), 303- [314]
as part of "Sandro Botticelli, Luca della Robbia: Two
Renaissance Studies by Walter Pater". Mosher supplied an
appreciative Introduction and included short extracts from the
"Conclusion" and the "Preface" to THE RENAISSANCE

In the Pater home were two lovely della Robbia plaques, blue and
white, approx. 9" in diameter.

14 Joachim du Bellay   (written) 1872

First printed in:
STUDIES IN THE HISTORY OF THE RENAISSANCE (1873) pp. 123-145
(see No. 16)

This essay was published by Thomas Bird Mosher (Portland,
Maine, U.S.A.) in The Bibelot, Vol. II (October 1896), 301 -
[328]. as "Joachim du Bellay: a Renaissance Study". Mosher
supplied a short eulogistic Introduction, and included a
sonnet "Joachim du Bellay" by Austin Dobson, also a short
extract from Ballads and Lyrics of Old France and a sonnet
"Joachim du Bellay" both by Andrew Lang.

In November 1870, June 1871 and July 1872 Pater was reading
Du Bellay: Oevres at the Bodleian Library.

15 Preface   (written) 1872

Written for and printed in:
STUDIES IN THE HISTORY OF THE RENAISSANCE (1873) pp. (vii) -
xiv. (see No. 16)

Thomas Bird Mosher (Portland, Maine, U.S.A.) published an
extract from this item ("It is in Italy in the fifteenth
century, that . . . many sided centralised, complete") in

16 STUDIES IN THE HISTORY OF THE RENAISSANCE   15 February 1873

———————————

This, Pater's first book, contained, in the order in which
they appeared in the book, the following essays:.

Preface	See No. 15
Aucassin and Nicolette	12
Pico della Mirandula	9
Sandro Botticelli	8
Luca della Robbia	13
The Poetry of Michelangelo	10
Lionardo da Vinci	7
Joachim du Bellay	14
Winckelmann	**5**
Conclusion	6

For a full description of this book, together with circumstances
of its publication, and later editions, see Section I b BOOKS, **1**

17 On Wordsworth   1 April 1874

———————————

The Fortnightly Review
No. LXXXVIII, Vol. XXI o.s., XV n.s. (1 April 1874)
pp. 456-465

———————————

The Fortnightly Review essay was thoroughly revised and, with
two extra paragraphs, appeared in:

APPRECIATIONS (15th November 1889), pp. 37-63, as
"Wordsworth". (see No. 71)

———————————

This essay in its various guises appeared in no less than seven
places: three times in periodicals and four times in books (see
Nos. 17, 61, 62, 71, 100, 101 and 103). Some are verbatim
copies, others show differences of arrangement and revision, but
all are from the Fortnightly Review root-stock, above.

A comparison of the versions and statement of their inter-
relationship will be found in Appendix b 3 "Wordsworth"

The Fortnightly Review
No. XCV,   Vol. XXII o.s., XVI n.s. (1 November 1874),
pp. 652-658

First printed in book form in:
APPRECIATIONS (1889), pp. 176-191
as "Measure for Measure". (see No. 71)

See No. 24: "The School of Giorgione" for an abortive proposal
to publish a volume containing "On 'Measure for Measure' " in
1878.

The manuscript of this essay is in the Folger Library, Washington
3, D.C. U.S.A.   It comprises 19 sheets.

19   "Renaissance in Italy: The Age of Despots"   31 July 1875
        by John Addington Symonds
        (London: Smith Elder & Co.   1875)

The Academy
Vol. VIII (July 31, 1875), pp. 105-106

First printed in book form in:
UNCOLLECTED ESSAYS (1903), pp. 1-12
Published by Thomas Bird Mosher (Portland, Maine, U.S.A.) in a
limited edition of 450 copies; the review entitled "Symonds's
Renaissance in Italy".   (see No. 101)

In Section I b BOOKS will be found a list of those known
writings by Walter Pater which, as with the above piece, do not
appear in either the Edition de Luxe of 1900/1901 or the New
Library Edition 1910

20   The Myth of Demeter and Persephone   (written) 1875

"A lecture delivered in substance at The Birmingham and Midland
Institute" (f.n.) on 29th November 1875

The Fortnightly Review, in two parts:
No. CIX, Vol. XXV o.s., XIX n.s. (1 January 1876), pp. 82-95
    CX   XXV o.s., XIX n.s. (1 February 1876),pp. 260-276
Littell's Living Age (Boston, Mass., U.S.A.)
No. 1654, Vol. CXXVIIIo.s., XIII n.s. (19 February 1876),
    pp. 480-488
No. 1662, Vol. CXXIX o.s., XIV n.s. (15 April 1876), pp. 152-
161

In 1878 Pater revised this, with two other essays - "A Study of
Dionysus" and "The Bacchanals of Euripides" (Nos. 22 and 28) -
"with the intention, apparently, of publishing them
collectively in a volume, an intention afterwards abandoned".
(see the Introduction by Charles L. Shadwell to GREEK STUDIES)
From the proofs then set up, and further corrected in manuscript, his literary executors printed the the essay in its
first edition in book form in:
GREEK STUDIES (1895), pp. 79-155 (see No. 97)

Extracts from this essay were published by Thomas Bird Mosher
(Portland, Maine, U.S.A.) in The Bibelot, Vol. V (June 1899),
183 - ⌊203⌋ as "Demeter and Persephone: Three Translations".
Mosher supplied a short introduction and included a poem on
the subject by George Meredith. The extracts were also
prefixed with a quotation from the essays: pp. 110-112
commencing: "The Worship of sorrow ! as Geothe called it . . .
at first sight painful and strange".
The extracts were, using page numbers from GREEK STUDIES:

    pp. 79 - 89   "The Song of Demeter"
       132 - 136   "Episode from Claudian's The Rape of
                     Proserpine"
       136 - 139   "Fragment from Ovid's Fasti"

The manuscript of this lecture is extant and a description will be
found in Section I c. LOCATION OF PUBLISHED MANUSCRIPTS

A.C. Benson (Walter Pater, 1906, p. 71) stated: "Pater said this
had been the most laborious and difficult work he had ever done".

21 Romanticism   November 1876

Macmillan's Magazine
No.CXX, Vol. XXXV (November 1876), pp. 64-70

First printed in book form in:
APPRECIATIONS (1889), pp. 243-264
as "Postcript"

The "Postcript" version shows a number of points of difference
from "Romanticism", and a short note on these will be found in
Section I b BOOKS - APPRECIATIONS

See No. 24: "The School of Giorgione" for an abortive proposal to
publish a volume containing "Romanticism" in 1878

22 A Study of Dionysus   1 December 1876
    I. The Spiritual Form of Fire and Dew

The Fortnightly Review
No. CXX, Vol. XXVI o.s., XX n.s. (1 December 1876), pp. 752-
772

In 1878, Pater revised this with three other essays - "The
Myth of Demeter and Persephone" (Two essays) and "The
Bacchanals of Euripides" (see Nos. 20 and 25) - "with the
intention, apparently, of publishing them collectively in a
volume, an intention afterwards abandoned" (see the Introduction of C.L. Shadwell to GREEK STUDIES). From the proofs
then set up, and further corrected in manuscript, his literary
executors printed the first edition of the essay in book form:
GREEK STUDIES (1895), pp. [1] - 48. (see No. 97)

The essay is numbered I, and finishes "(to be continued)". The
second part of the essay is "The Bacchanals of Euripides" (see No.
25) which appeared in Macmillan's Magazine, May 1889. This is
indicated by the context of the first page of the latter essay, and
by C.L. Shadwell's observation on p. vi of the Preface to GREEK
STUDIES: "The Bacchanals of Euripides" must have been written
about the same time, as a sequel to the "Study of Dionysus".

A further item of information about this article is that in Oct.
1878 when Pater proposed to Alexander Macmillan to include it in a
forthcoming volume of essays (never published) he entitled it:
        The Myth of Dionysus - - -
             1. The spiritual form of fire and dew
             2. The Bacchanals of Euripides

The importance that Pater attached to this essay can be judges
from the fact that he later proposed to call the volume Dionysus
and other Studies

23 THE RENAISSANCE: STUDIES IN ART AND POETRY   24 May 1877

Second edition of:
STUDIES IN THE HISTORY OF THE RENAISSANCE (1873) see No. 16

The contents, in order of the book, are:

No. 12 "Two early French Stories" was entitled "Aucassin and Nicolette" in the 1873 edition.

"Pico della Mirandula" becomes "Pico della Mirandola"

"Conclusion", which appeared as the final essay of the first edition, was now omitted.

For a full description of this book and particulars of its publication see Section I b BOOKS: 1 THE RENAISSANCE

---

24 The School of Giorgione   1 October 1877

The Fortnightly Review
No. CXXX, Vol. XXVIII o.s., XXII n.s. (1 October 1877), pp. 526-538

First printed in book form in:
THE RENAISSANCE: STUDIES IN ART AND POETRY
(3rd edition) 1888, pp. 135-161 (see No. 51)

This essay was published by Thomas Bird Mosher (Portland, Maine Portland, U.S.A.) in The Bibelot, Vol. IV (September 1898), pp. 285-[315]. Mosher supplied a short introduction, and included a sonnet: "For a Venetian Pastoral by Giorgione(In the Louvre)" by Dante Gabriel Rossetti.

Pater mentions the Giorgione essay in a letter to William Sharp
(Papers Critical and Reminiscent (Heinemann) 1912, pp. 210-211)
dated November 5, 1882: "As to the paper on Giorgione which I
read to you in manuscript, I find I have by me a second copy of the
proof which I have revised and sent by this post, and hope you will
kindly accept it. It was reprinted some time ago, when I thought
of collecting that and other papers into a volume."
On pp. 205-207, Sharp describes Pater reading to him: "When he
read, Pater spoke in a low voice, rather hesitatingly at first, and
sometimes almost constrainedly. Soon, however, he became absorbed;
then his face would light up as with an inner glow, he would lean
forward and though his voice neither quickened nor intensified
there was a new vibration. Occasionally, he would move his right
hand slowly, with an undulating motion."
Sharpe writes: "The copy of Giorgione essay alluded to in this
letter was one of several essays printed at the Clarendon Press in
Oxford at Pater's own cost. I asked him once why, particularly as
his was so clear and beautiful a handwriting, he went to this heavy
expense when he did not mean to publish (and in some instances the
 type was distributed after a few copies had been printed); to
which he replied that though he could, and did, revise often and
scrupulously in manuscript, he could never adequately disentangle
his material from the intellectual light in which it had been
conceived, until he saw it in the vivid and unsparing actuality of
type. This copy , besides its autograph inscription and textual
corrections, bears the circular stamp of the Clarendon Press,
November 12, 1878; so it was printed three years before I heard it
from Manuscript, and more than ten years before it was published in
book form along with other papers. As its pagination is from page
157 to page 184, its author must have had quite a large volume
printed at the Clarendon Press". (The Clarendon Press, alas, have
not been able to find any copies of these trial printings) Sharp
nowhere mentions the Fortnightly Review printing.

Pater wrote to Alexander Macmillan on October 1, 1878 (LWP No. 52)
proposing that a volume of his Fortnightly Review essays should
appear as a book, and in the list of contents "The School of
Giorgione" appears as the first item, indeed Pater proposed to call
the volume The School of Giorgione, and other studies. By Nov.
[1878] he had changed his mind and decided to abandon the project
even though Macmillan's had set the book up in type and sent him
the proofs (LWP no. 55)
The list of contents which Pater supplied for the proposed volume
was as follows:

> The School of Giorgione
> Wordsworth
> The Myth of Demeter -
>   1. The Homeric Hymn
>   2. Demeter and Persephone
> The Myth of Dionysus -
>   1. The spiritual form of fire and dew
>   2. The Bacchanals of Euripides
> Romanticism
> On 'Love's Labour Lost'

On 'Measure for Measure'
The character of the humourist - Charles Lamb

25 The Bacchanals of Euripides   (written) prior to 1 October 1878

Macmillan's Magazine
No. XXXLV, Vol. LX (May 1889), pp. 63-72

First printed in book form in:
GREEK STUDIES (1895), pp. 49-78   (see No. 97)

There is some doubt as to the year when this essay was written.
While in the preface to MISCELLANEOUS STUDIES, Charles L. Shadwell
gives 1878, in the preface to GREEK STUDIES he says that it must
have been written about the same time as the "Study of Dionysus"
1876 (see No. 22).
It was certainly ready by 1 October 1878 as Pater proposed to
include it in a projected book of his essays (see "The School of
Giorgione" No. 24 above).

In the Preface to GREEK STUDIES Shadwell also stated that this
essay, "was reprinted without alteration, prefixed to Dr. Tyrrell's
edition of the Bacchae" (The Bacchanals of Euripides with a
revision of the text and a commentary by Robert Yelverton Tyrell:
1892), but he was mistaken.

26 On "Love's Labours Lost"   (written) 1878

Macmillan's Magazine
No. CCCXIV, Vol. LIII (December 1885), pp. 89-91

The Eclectic Magazine (New York, U.S.A.)
Vol. XLIII n.s., CVI o.s. (February 1886), pp. 234-237

First printed in book form in:
APPRECIATIONS (1889), pp. 167-175
as "Love's Labours Lost", and there dated 1878

This paper was read before the New Shakespere Society and the
following extract is taken from the Transactions:

    New Shakespere Society: Transactions
    Forty-second meeting, April 13, 1878
    Hy Courthope Bowen, Esq. (Treasurer) in the chair.

The papers read were:-

I. "On Love's Labour's Lost" by W.H. Pater, Esq.
Fellow and Tutor of Brasenose College, Oxford
II. "Some Remarks concerning the Introductory Scene of
the Second Part of <u>Henry IV</u>" by Prof. Hagenor of
Oldenbury.

III. "On Hamlet" as the greatest of Shakespeare's Plays
. . . by Rev. M. Wynell Mayow, B.D.

See No. 24: "The School of Giorgione" for an abortive proposal to
publish a volume containing "On Love's Labour Lost" in 1878

27 Imaginary Portraits   (written) April 1878
1. The Child in the House

<u>Macmillan's Magazine</u>
No. CCXXVI, Vol. XXXVIII (August 1878), pp. 313-321

<u>Littell's Living Age</u> (Boston, U.S.A.)
No. 1785, Vol. CXXVIII o.s., XXIII n.s. (31 August 1878),
pp. 566-573

First edition in book form:
AN IMAGINARY PORTRAIT by Walter Pater
Printed by H. Daniels at his Private Press at Oxford (June
1894) in a limited edition of 250 copies (see No. 95)
The Daniel book was probably one of the few books to appear at
a public fete and was the first appearance of this item in
book form. It was however a truly private venture, printed
by an amateur, though a highly accomplished one.

First public edition in book form in this country (England) in
MISCELLANEOUS STUDIES (18th October 1895), pp. 171-197 (see
No. 98)

This Portrait was published however as a separate book twice
in U.S.A. in 1895, and a question of priority of edition
arises. The two editions were:

> The Child in the House: An Imaginary Portrait
> Copeland and Day: Boston: 1895 [September]
>
> A Child in the House: An Imaginary Portrait
> Thomas Bird Mosher: Portland Maine: 1895 [November ?]
> This was a limited edition of 425 copies, 44 pages on
> Japan vellum. It was in Mosher's Brocade series.
> Mosher republished this in his Vest Pocket series, XVII,
> 1909, printed on both Van Gelder handmade paper and on
> Japan vellum.

The Copeland and Day book was printed in July 1895 and
published by the early part of September 1895. <u>The Nation</u>

(New York), LXI (5 September 1895), p. 170, listed it in
"Books of the week" and the same journal on 18th September 1895
p. 213 advertised it as "just published". The price was
$1.50. This is probably the first <u>public</u> appearance of <u>The
Child in the House</u> in book form.

With regard to the Mosher edition, the Colophon, p. 46,
states "Four hundred and twenty copies of this book have been
printed on Japan Vellum and type distributed in the month of
September, A.D. MDCCCXCV, at the press of George D. Loreung,
Portland, Maine. (A second edition was printed in November
1895). The actual publication would be a little later,
probably in November 1895, when it was advertised in <u>The
Chap-Book</u>. At least 14 editions of this book were published
in this series, the 14th being in December 1908.

<u>The Child in the House</u> was also published by Dodd, Mead & Co.
New York in 1909

On April 17, 1878, Pater wrote to George Groves, then editor of
<u>Macmillan's Magazine</u>, saying: "I send you by the post an M.S.
entitled <u>The House and the Child</u>, and should be pleased if you
would like to have it for Macmillan's Magazine. It is not, as
you may perhaps fancy, the first part of a work of fiction, but it
is meant to be complete in itself; though the first of a series
as I hope, with some real kind of sequence in them, and mean
readers, as they might do on seeing a portrait, to begin
speculating - - what came of him ?" (<u>LWP</u> No. 47)

At first, Pater asked for the article to appear without his
signature, but later, on Groves's proposal, consented to have it
restored (June 11th. <u>LWP</u>. No. 50)

This is an appropriate place in which to mention the interest in
Walter Pater shown in Japanese literary circles. At the
University of Tokyo there is a Pater Society, with a very healthy
membership. It meets monthly and publishes a monthly journal
containing essays by members and notes from book reviews on a
world-wide basis. Members of the Society have visited England
in recent years, and it may be of interest to append a note on a
version of "The Child in the House" by two Japanese scholars.
(Ms Brasenose College, Oxford).

W.H. Pater

THE CHILD IN THE HOUSE

edited with notes by
S. Kawaguchi and K. Takeda (and presented by K.
Takeda)

Sankaido, 1960

Paper back, octavo.

Introduction (J)

Text (E)

Notes (E. & J.)

Pater: a short biography (J)

Chronological Table (E)

Bibliographical note   I (E)
                       II (J)

28 The Character of the Humourist: 1 October 1878
    Charles Lamb

The Fortnightly Review
No. CXLII, Vol. XXX o.s., XXIV n.s. (1 October 1878), pp. 466-474

First printed in book form in:
APPRECIATIONS (1889), pp. 107-126
as "Charles Lamb"   (see No. 71)

Thomas B. Mosher (Portland, Maine, U.S.A.) printed this essay
in The Bibelot, Vol. XII, pp. 221-243 (July 1906) as "Charles
Lamb: An Appreciation"

See No. 24: "The School of Giorgione" for an abortive proposal
to publish a volume containing: "The character of the
Humourist - Charles Lamb", in 1878

Aspects of Wilde by Vincent O'Sullivan (Constable) 1936, has the
following passage, pp. 11-13:

"Walter Pater he Wilde thought, was far too sensitive to the
"Criticisms of people not fit to tie his shoes.   Once at
"Oxford, he came on Pater brooding on an article which
"attempted to turn into ridicule his essay on Charles Lamb.
"The article was entitled: "Lamb - and Mint Sauce" and was
"written by H.D. Traill, a writer of considerable repute.
"Wilde was dumbfounded.   He said his estimate of Pater as a
"man altered from that moment.   'Just imagine ! Pater !   I
"could not conceive how one could be Pater and yet be
"susceptible to the insults of the lowest form of Journalism !
"In that is all the difference between Pater and the
"vulgariser of Pater. . . . "

29 Imaginary Portraits   (written) 1878 ?
    2. An English Poet
        by Walter Pater, edited by May Ottley

The Fortnightly Review
Vol. CXXIX (1 April 1931), pp. 433-448
(pp. 433-435 contains Mrs Ottley's introduction;
435-448 Pater's text)

This essay was edited and published with an introduction by Mrs
May Ottley, who was at that time (1931) the holder of the
copyright of Pater's works. The Introduction is full of interest
and is given in full in Appendix c. 2

There are no means of saying with certitude when the piece was
written. It must certainly, by its title, have followed
"Imaginary Portraits I. The Child in the House" (see No. 27)
which was published in Macmillan's Magazine in August 1878, and
probably drafted before October 1885when "A Prince of Court
Painters" (see No. 37) was published, for that was the first in
his IMAGINARY PORTRAUTS. M. d'Hangest in his Walter Pater:
l'homme et l'oeuvre (Paris: 1961) has reviewed the internal
evidence thoroughly in a note (5) on pp. 366-367 of his first
volume. He regards "An English Poet" as a bridge between "The
Child in the House" and "Marius the Epicurean" (March 1885), and
effectively points to a number of correspondences between the
"English Poet" and the early chapters of Marius. He considers
that Pater abandoned this item only to represent many of its
themes in Marius. As that book was certainly commenced by 1881,
and probably before then, the date is narrowed down to the years
1878-1880 inclusive. Lawrence Evans suggests that Pater was
working on this portrait in 1878 (LWP p. 35 n. 2)

30 The Beginnings of Greek Sculpture   1 February &
        I. The Heroic Age of Greek Art   1 March 1880
        II. The Age of Graven Images

The Fortnightly Review
    I. No. CLVIII, II. No. CLIX, Vol. XXXIII o.s., XXVII n.s.
(1 February 1880) pp. 190-207 and (1 March 1880), 422-434

First printed in book form in:
GREEK STUDIES (1895),   pp. 194-233;   234-262   see no. 97

31 The Marbles of Aegina   1 April 1880

The Fortnightly Review
No. CIX, Vol. XXXIII o.s., XXVII n.s. (1 April 1880), pp. 540-
    548

First printed in book form in:
GREEK STUDIES (1895) 263-282   See No. 97

The Harvard Library of Harvard University, U.S.A. have a Pater
manuscript: "The Marbles of Aegina", unsigned, n.p., n.d., 16s
(16p) "Lecture which preceded the larger published essay of this
title."

Pater stated that the marbles were purchased by the Crown Prince,
afterwards King Louis I of Bavaria, but behind that narration lies
an attractive episode and an eccentric personality.   Charles
Robert Cockerell (1788-1863), a direct descendent of Samuel Pepys,
set out for Greece when 22 years old, with £200 in his pocket.
After spending 3 months in Constantinople, sketching palaces,
houses and mosques, he proceded to Athens, "then a small and
squalid town with no proper hotel", then to the island of Aegina,
where he and 3 others pitched their tents and stayed for 3 months.
He discovered the fragments of statuary which later came to be
known as the "Aegina Marbles" "and most shockingly smuggled them
out of Greece at night" eventually to be bought at auction by the
King of Bavaria.
He became a very respected architect: 1819 Surveyor to St. Pauls;
1833 Architect to the Bank of England;   architect for the
Ashmolean Museum and the Taylorian Institution, Oxford; R.A.
1836;   President R.I.B.A. in 1860 (information from the R.I.B.A.
Journal).
I wonder if in later days he told the story of the commandmant of
the Acropolis (then a fortress) who offered him a gift if he would
take it away ? "So he arrived at midnight with a cart, and the
commandmant pitched down to him from aloft a huge marble block
forming part of the South frieze of the Parthenon (somewhat
battered and now in the British Museum). "

---

32 Samuel Taylor Coleridge   1880

First appeared as an introductory essay to a selection of
Coleridge's poems in:
The English Poete: Selections
with critical introductions by various writers and a general
introduction by Matthew Arnold.   Edited by Thomas Humphrey
Ward, M.A. late Fellow of Brasenose College, Oxford, 4 vols.
(Macmillan and Co. (1880-1883)

The Pater essay appeared in Vol. IV (1880), pp. 102-114

Four volumes were published in 1880 and a fifth volume
"Browning to Rupert Brooke" in 1918.

Pater also contributed the introduction to "Dante Gabriel
Rossetti" for this anthology.   (see No. 34)

This essay first appeared in a Pater publication in:

APPRECIATIONS (1889), pp. 64-106 (part). (see No. 71)
In that volume it was revised and included as the latter part
of the essay "Coleridge". For a note on the various inter-
related articles on Coleridge see Appendix b. 4. Coleridge.

The manuscript of this essay is at Harvard University.

A set of The English Poets, first editions, with each title page
signed "Walter Pater" was found in a bookcase in the Pater home.

The English Poets was in many ways a model of what a major
anthology should be. In order that adequate and sympathetic
treatment of each should be given, Humphrey Ward fitted the critic
to the poet, engaging a number of brilliant writers for the
introductions. They included T. Humphrey Ward himself; his wife
Mary Augusta Ward; T. Arnold; W.E. Henley; Andrew Lang; A.C.
Bradley; Ernest Dowden; George Saintsbury; W.W. Ward; Austin
Dobson; Mark Pattison; A.C. Swinburne; J.A. Symonds and
Matthew Arnold. The later also provided a general Introduction,
and it proved to be one of his major essays.

33 "Love in Idleness"   7 March 1883
          [unsigned review]

          Love in Idlesness: A Volume of Poems
          Kegan Paul, Trench & Co. (1883)

          This is a volume of poems by H.C. Beeching, J.B. Nicholls
          and J.W. Mackail, published anonymously

          ―――――――――――

          This little known review has not been reprinted in any form,
          and is not mentioned in any list or bibliography.

          In Section I b BOOKS will be found a list of those known
          writings of Walter Pater which do not appear in either the
          Edition de Luxe of 1900/1901 or the New Library Edition 1910

34 Dante Gabriel Rossetti   1883

          ―――――――――――

          First published as an introductory essay to a selection of
          Rossetti's poems in:
          The English Poets: Selections
          with critical introductions by various writers and a general
          introduction by Matthew Arnold.   Edited by Thomas Humphrey
          Ward, M.A. late Fellow of Brasenose College, Oxford. 4 vols.
          (Macmillan and Co. 1883)

          Pater's essay appeared in Vol. IV pp. 633-641 (2nd edition).
          It was not included in the first (1880) edition as Rossetti
          was then alive.   21

There is a letter written by Pater to Humohrey Ward (<u>LWP</u> No. 75)
dated March 5th (1883) regarding this essay in which he said:
"Many thanks for your letter which I have been unable to answer
before.   I think I shall be able to do what you propose for your
new edition, but can't feel quite certain for a day or two, if <u>not</u>
I will let you know when you come to Oxford . . . "

This essay first appeared in a Pater publication in:
<u>APPRECIATIONS</u> (1889), pp. 228-242. (see No. 71)

Thomas Bird Mosher (Portland, Maine, U.S.A.) published this
essay in <u>The Bibelot</u>, Vol. V. (October 1899), pp. 303-[338]
"Two Appreciations: I Aesthetic Poetry. II Dante Gabriel
Rossetti".

The two versions (Anthology and <u>APPRECIATIONS</u>) differ only in
slight revisions, e.g. Ward. p. 639: Were there indeed ages ?";
APPRECIATIONS p. 239: "Have there, in very deed, been ages ?"
(Pater's revisions were usually on the expansive side).

For a note on <u>The English Poets</u> see No. 32 "Samuel Taylor
Coleridge".

Macmillan's paid Pater £15 for this Introduction.

Pater possessed a copy of <u>Ballads and Sonnets</u> (1881) by Dante
Gabriel Rossetti.

The manuscript of this essay is in the library of a private
collector, U.S.A.

35 "The English School of Painting"   25 February 1885
        [signed review]

        <u>The English School of Painting</u> by Ernest Chesnau. trans
        by L.N. Etherington with a Preface by Professor Ruskin
        (1885). Cassell & Co.

        _____

        <u>The Oxford Magazine</u>
        Vol. III, No. 6 (25 February 1885), p. 113

        _____

This little known article has not been reprinted in any form and is
not mentioned in any list or bibliography.
In Section I b BOOKS will be found a list of those known writings
of Walter Pater which do not appear in either the Edition de Luxe
of 1900/1901 or the New Library Edition 1910

It may be of interest to note that Pater owned a 4 volume set of
the 3rd edition of <u>Anecdotes of Painting in England,</u> collected by
the late George Vertue and now published by Horace Walpole (1782).

36 MARIUS THE EPICUREAN: HIS SENSATIONS AND IDEAS 2 vols.
4 March 1885

This was written as a book, and there is no prior printing
in any other form.

For a full description of this work and particulars of its
publication, see Section I b BOOKS, 2 Marius the Epicurean.

37 A Prince of Court Painters: October 1885
        Extracts from an old French Journal

Macmillan's Magazine
No. CCXII, Vol. LII (October 1885), pp. 401-414

Littell's Living Age (Boston, U.S.A.)
No. 2160, Vol. CLXVII o.s., LII n.s. (14 November 1885),
    pp. 421-431

The Eclectic Magazine (New York: U.S.A.)
Vol. CV o.s., XLII n.s., (December 1885), pp. 782-794

First printed in book form in:
IMAGINARY PORTRAITS (1887), pp. [1] - 48

This portrait was published in a separate volume:
A PRINCE OF COURT PAINTERS: AN IMAGINARY PORTRAIT
by Thomas Bird Mosher (Portland, Maine, U.S.A.) in his
Brocade series (August 1898). It is a 12mo volume, of 64
pages, Japan vellum, printed by George D. Loring, in a Limited
Edition of 425 copies. A second edition was published in
September of the same year, and a third edition in July 1906
It is the only known edition of this portrait as a separate
volume

38 MARIUS THE EPICUREAN: HIS SENSATIONS AND IDEAS 2 vols.
        Second Edition   12 November 1885

For a full description of this work, and particulars of its
publication, see Section I b BOOKS, 2 Marius the Epicurean

39 Four Books for Students of English Literature   17 February 1886
      [unsigned review]

        Saintsbury: Specimens of English Prose from Malory to Macaulay
        Minto: Characteristics of English Poets
        Austin Dobson: Selections from Steele
        Ainger: Mrs Leicester's School, and other writings in
          Prose and Verse

        _____

        The Guardian
        No. 2098, Vol. XLI (17 February 1886), pp. 246-247

        _____

        First printed in book form in:
        ESSAYS FROM THE 'GUARDIAN' pp. 1 - 18
        Printed for Private Circulation at the Chiswick Press
          (1896), 100 copies only   (see No. 100)

        _____

        This was the first of a series of unsigned reviews which Pater
        Contributed to The Guardian. Information regarding their
        publication will be found in Section I b BOOKS No. 10: Essays
        from the 'Guardian'

40 "Amiels Journal: The Journal Intime of Henri-Frédéric Amiel"
      Translated, with an introduction and notes, by Mrs
      Humphrey Ward, 2 vols. (Macmillan's) 1886.   17 March 1886
      [unsigned review]

        _____

        The Guardian
        No. 2102, Vol. XLI (17 March 1886), pp. 406-407

        _____

        First edition in book form in:
        ESSAYS FROM THE 'GUARDIAN'   pp. 19-41 as
        "Amiel's 'Journal Intime'. "
        Printed for Private Circulation at the Chiswick Press
          (1896), 100 copies only   (see No. 100)

        _____

        For a note on the Guardian articles see Section I b BOOKS No. 10:
        Essays from the 'Guardian'

        A.C. Benson on pp. 199-200 of his Walter Pater (1906), quotes
        from a letter sent by Pater to Mrs Ward, dated 23 December 1885,
        on receiving from her as a Christmas gift her newly published
        translation of Amiel's Journal. This is a very important and
        intersting letter, (quoted in LWP No. 95)

                                24

Macmillan's Magazine
No. 317, Vol. LIII (March 1886), pp. 348-360

Littell's Living Age (Boston, U.S.A.)
No. 2180, Vol. CLXIX o.s., LIV n.s., (April 1886), pp. 28-38

First printed in book form in:
IMAGINARY PORTRAITS (1887), pp. [89] - 133   (see No. 47)

This portrait was published in a separate volume:
SEBASTIAN VAN STORCK: AN IMAGINARY PORTRAIT by Thomas Bird
Mosher (Portland, Maine, U.S.A.), in his 'Brocade' series,
August 1890, 12mo, 60 pages, printed by George D. Loring,
Portland, on Japan Vellum, in a Limited Edition of 425 copies.
This was the first publication in a separate volume.
A second edition was published in September of the same year.

Macmillan's Magazine
No. 319, Vol. LIV (May 1886), pp. 5-18

Littell's Living Age
No. 2190, Vol. CLXIX o.s., LIV n.s. (12 June 1886), pp. 643-654

The Eclectic Magazine
No. 6, Vol. CVI o.s., XLIII n.s. (June 1886), pp. 841-853

First printed in book form in:
APPRECIATIONS (1889), pp. 127-166   (see No. 71)

Thomas B. Mosher (Portland, Maine, U.S.A.) reprinted in The
Bibelot, Vol. XIX, No. 12 (December 1913), pp. 399-405, part of
Pater's essay on Sir Thomas Browne.   This was prefatory to a
reprint of the last chapter of Hydriotaphia.   The portion
reprinted was from p. 157 (book version), commencing:
"Palingenesis, resurrection effected by orderly prescription .
. . to (page 162) "so many of his single sentences are made to
fall upon the ear".

The manuscript of this essay is in the library of a private
collector, U.S.A.

Macmillan's Magazine
No. 324, Vol. LIV (October 1886), pp. 413-423

Littell's Living Age (Boston, U.S.A.)
No. 2212, Vol. CLXXI o.s., LVI n.s. (November 1886), pp.
419-427

The Eclectic Magazine (N.Y., U.S.A.)
No. 6 Vol. CVII o.s., XLIV n.s. (December 1886), pp. 746-756

First printed in book form in:
IMAGINARY PORTRAITS (1887), pp. [49] - 88   (see No. 47)

This portrait was published in a separate volume as:
DENYS L'AUXERROIS: AN IMAGINARY PORTRAIT by Thomas Bird Mosher
(Portland, Maine, E.S.A.) in his 'Brocade' series, in July 1898
12mo, 54 pages, Japan Vellum, printed by George D. Loring,
Portland, in a Limited Edition of 425 copies.   This is the
only known edition of this publication in a separate volume.
A second edition was published in September of the same year.

44 English at the Universities   27 November 1886

Pall Mall Gazette
Vol. XLIV (Saturday, November 27, 1886), pp. 1 - 2

This article has not been listed in any bibliography, or reprinted
in any volume of Pater's writings (see however LWP No. 192 where it
was printed as a letter).

In Section I b BOOKS will be found a list of those known writings of
Walter Pater which do not appear in either the Edition de Luxe of
1900/1901 or the New Library Edition 1910

This is one of a series of articles on the Petition headed "Oxford
Nov. 2, 1886" addressed to the Hebdomadal Council to urge the
foundation of a School of Modern Language and Literature.   The
Pall Mall Gazette took a great interest in the proposal, one which
caused great controversy at the time, and printed articles from no
less than 29 well-known people, including John Bright, Archdeacon
Farrer, William E. Gladstone, Professor Huxley, John Addington
Symonds, F.W.H. Myers and Thomas H. Warren.   The School of
English Literature was not established until 1893.
The question is discussed at length in Sir Charles Firth's book
The School of English Language and Literature (Oxford and London),
1908.

45 M. Feuillet's 'La Morte'   December 1886
    ⌊unsigned review⌋

    Macmillan's Magazine
    No. 326, Vol. LIV (December 1886), pp. 97-105

    First printed in book form in:
    APPRECIATIONS, second edition (1890), pp. 219-240 (see No. 78)
    as Feuillet's "La Morte"

46 Duke Carl of Rosenmold   May 1887

    Macmillan's Magazine
    No. 331, Vol. LVI (May 1887), pp. 19-31

    Littell's Living Age (Boston, U.S.A.)
    No. 2243, Vol. CLXXIII o.s., LVIII n.s. (18 June 1998), pp.
      743-752

    The Eclectic Magazine (New York, U.S.A.)
    No. 1, Vol. CIX o.s., XLVI n.s. (July 1887), pp. 20-31

    First printed in book form in:
    IMAGINARY PORTRAITS (1887), ⌊135⌋ - 180   (see No. 47)

    This portrait was published in a separate volume:
    DUKE CARL OF ROSENMOLD: AN IMAGINARY PORTRAIT, by Thomas Bird
    Mosher (Portland, Maine, U.S.A.), in his 'Brocade' series,
    August 1898, 12mo., 60 pages, at the press of George D. Loring,
    Portland, on Japan Vellum, in a limited edition of 425 copies.
    A second edition was published in September of the same year.
    This is the only known edition of this publication in a
    separate volume.

47 IMAGINARY PORTRAITS   24 May 1887

    Contents:
            Sebastian van Storck   No. 41

            A Prince of Court Painters   37

            Denys l'Auxerrois   43

            Duke Carl of Rosenmold   46

    A full description of this book and subsequent editions will be.

48 Vernon Lee's 'Juvenalia'   5 August 1887
        [unsigned review]

        "Juvenalia: Being a Second Series on Sundry Aesthetical
        Questions" by Vernon Lee. Two Volumes. (London: T. Fisher
        Unwin)

        _____

        Pall Mall Gazette
        Vol. XLV (5 August 1887), p. 5

        _____

This has not been reprinted in any other form and is not listed or
mentioned in any book-list or bibliography. It is attributed to
Pater on the following grounds:
In Vernon Lee's Letters (1937), a privately printed volume of 30
copies, with a preface by her friend and literary executor, Miss
Irene Cooper Willis, a letter to Miss Lee's mother, headed "Casa
Pater, 30 July 1887" says, inter alia: "I don't think I have any
further news except that Pater has written a review of Juvenalia for
the Pall Mall, which hasn't yet appeared." The Pall Mall review
listed above did appear 6 days later. The style of writing is
similar to Pater's.

In Section I b BOOKS will be found a list of those known writings of
Walter Pater which do not appear in either the Edition de Luxe of
1900/1901 or the New Library Edition 1910

49 "An Introduction to the Study of Browning"   9 November 1887
        By Arthur Symons (Cassells)
        [unsigned review]

        _____

        The Guardian
        No. 2188, Vol. XLII (9 November 1887), pp. 1709-1710

        _____

        First printed in book form in:
        ESSAYS FROM THE 'GUARDIAN' (1896), pp. 43-56
        as "Browning".   Printed for Private Circulation at the
        Chiswick Press.   100 copies only   (see No. 100)
        For the Guardian articles, see note on No. 39.

50　M. Lemaitre's "Serenus, and other Tales"　　　　　　November 1887
　　　　[unsigned review]

　　　　　　　　　　　　──────────────

　　　Macmillan's Magazine
　　　No. 337, Vol. LVII (November 1887), pp. 71-80

　　　　　　　　　　　　──────────────

　　　First printed in book form in:
　　　UNCOLLECTED ESSAYS (1903), pp. 13-48
　　　Published in a limited edition of 450 copies by Thomas Bird
　　　Mosher, (Portland, Maine, U.S.A.).　　(see No. 101)

　　　This review was also published in:
　　　SKETCHES AND REVIEWS　(1919)
　　　edited by Albert Mordell, published by Boni and Liberight,
　　　New York.　　(see No. 103)

51　THE RENAISSANCE STUDIES IN ART AND POETRY　　　January 1888

　　　Third Edition of
　　　STUDIES IN THE HISTORY OF THE RENAISSANCE (1873)　(See No. 16)

　　　　　　　　　　　　──────────────

The contents, in order of the book, are:

Preface	See No. 15
Two Early French Stories	12
Pico della Mirandola	9
Sandro Botticelli	8
Luca della Robbia	13
The Poetry of Michelangelo	10
Leonardo da Vinci	7
The School of Giorgione	24
Joachim de Bellay	14
Winckelmann	5
Conclusion	6

"The School of Giorgione" appeared here in book form for the first
time

"Conclusion", which was omitted from the second edition, was
restored in this and later editions.

For a full description of this book see Section I b BOOKS, No. 1
THE RENAISSANCE

52 "Robert Elsmere"   28 March 1888
        By Mrs Humphrey Ward (Smith & Elder) (Communicated)
        [Unsigned review]

The Guardian
No. 2208, Vol. XLIII (28 March 1888), pp. 468-469

First printed in book form in:
ESSAYS FROM THE 'GUARDIAN' (1896), pp. 57-76,
as "Robert Elsmere".   Printed for Private Circulation at the
Chiswick Press.   (see No. 100)
For a note on the Guardian articles see No. 39

A month before the publication of this review, Pater wrote to Mrs.
Ward to say: "One brief word of congratulation on having brought
your long labour to so worthy a conclusion as I feel R.E. to be.
I am reading it with very great interest and readiness, and shall
soon have finished it, and then hope you will kindly read my longer
observations about it.   It is a chef d'oeuvre after its kind, and
justifies the care you have devoted to it". (26 February 1888: see
LWP No. 123)

53 - 57 Gaston de Latour   June-October 1888

Macmillan's Magazine
Nos. 334-338, Vol. LVIII:

Chapter I   "A Clerk in Orders"   (June 1888), 152-160

        II "I had almost said even as they"
                                            (July 1888), 222-229

       III "Modernity"   (Aug. 1888), 258-266

        IV "Peach-Blossom and Wine"   (Sept. 1888), 393-400

         V "Suspended Judgment"   (Oct. 1888), 472-480

First printed in book form in:
GASTON DE LATOUR: AN UNFINISHED ROMANCE (1896), (see No. 99)
as the first five chapters of that book.

        Chapter 1 A Clark in orders   pp.   1-31

             II   Our Lady's Church   32-59

            III   Modernity   60-90

             IV   Peach-Blossom and Wine   91-113

              V   Suspended Judgment   114-144

The manuscripts of these essays, together with that of chapter VII of the book, are in the Berg Collection, New York Public Library. For a description of these manuscripts and those of the as yet unpublished chapters of Gaston, see Section I b BOOKS, No. 9: GASTON DE LATOUR

58 Their Majesties' Servants   27 June 1888
    [unsigned review]

    "Annals of the English Stage, from Thomas Betterton to
    Edmund Keen" by Doctor Doran F.S.A. Edited and revised by
    Robert W. Lowe (John V. Nimmo)

    The Guardian
    No. 22221, Vol. XLIII (27 June 1888), pp. 948-949

    First printed in book form in:
    ESSAYS FROM THE 'GUARDIAN' (1896), pp. 77-96
    Printed for Private Circulation at the Chiswick Press (see
    No. 100)
    For a note on the Guardian articles see No. 39

59 The Life and Letters of Flaubert   25 August 1888
    Review:
    "Correspondance: Premiere Serie ; 1830/1850 (Paris)

    Pall Mall Gazette
    Vol. XLVIII (25 August 1888), pp. 1-2

    This review was later expanded to become the essay:
    "Style" Fortnightly Review (December 1888). (see No. 60)

    Apart from the above essay the first appearance in book form
    was in:
    UNCOLLECTED ESSAYS (1903), pp. 49-64.
    Published by Thomas Bird Mosher (Portland, Maine, U.S.A.)
    in a limited edition of 450 copies. (see No. 101)

    It was also published in:
    SKETCHES AND REVIEWS (1919), edited by Albert Mordell and
    published by Boni and Liveright (New York). (see No. 103)

Pater possessed a copy of the following book:

Gustave Flaubert. Trois Contes. 2nd edition 1877
(signed "Walter Pater" on the half-title)

60 Style   December 1888

_____

The Fortnightly Review
No.CCLXIV Vol. L o.s., XLIV n.s. (December 1888), pp. 728-743

Littell's Living Age (Boston, U.S.A.)
No. 2323, Vol. CLXXX o.s., LIV n.s. (5 January 1889), pp. 3-13

_____

First printed in book form in:
APPRECIATIONS (1889), pp. 1-36   (see No. 71)

_____

This essay was founded on the review of "The Life and Letters of
Flaubert" - see No. 59

61 The Complete Poetical Works of Wordsworth   26 January 1889
         with an introduction by John Morley
         (Macmillan & Co.)
    The Recluse by William Wordsworth
         (same publishers)
    Selections from Wordsworth by William Knight
         and other members of the Wordsworth Society
         with preface and notes (Kegan Paul, Trench & Co.)

         [unsigned review]

_____

The Athenaeum
No. 3196 (26 January 1889), pp. 109-110

_____

First printed in book form in:
UNCOLLECTED ESSAYS (1903), pp. 65-76
Published by Thomas Bird Mosher (Portland, Maine, U.S.A.) in a
limited edition of 450 copies (see No. 101)

This review was also published in:
SKETCHES AND REVIEWS (1919)
Edited by Albert Mordell and published by Boni and Liveright,
New York.   (see No. 103)

_____

There are three periodical essays by Pater on Wordsworth - see also
Nos. 17 and 62 - all of which are related.   They were published by

Pater and others in four different books: see Nos. 71, 100, 101 and
103.

A comparison of the versions and a statement of their inter-
relationship will be found in Appendix b 3 "Wordsworth"

62   "The Complete Poetical Works of William   27 February 1889
         Wordsworth" with an Introduction by
         John Morley.   Macmillans
      "The Recluse" By William Wordsworth. Macmillans
      "Selections from Wordsworth". By William Knight
         and other members of the Wordsworth Society.
         With Preface and Notes.   Kegan Paul.

      [unsigned review]

      ────────────────

      The Guardian
      No. 2256, Vol. XLIV (27 February 1889), pp. 317-318

      ────────────────

      First printed in book form in:
      ESSAYS FROM THE 'GUARDIAN' (1896), pp. 97-114
      as "Wordsworth".
      Printed for Private Circulation at the Chiswick Press.
      100 copies only   (see No. 100)

      For a note on the Guardian articles see No. 39

      ────────────────

There are three periodical essays by Pater on Wordsworth — see also
Nos. 17 and 61 — all of which are related.   They were published by
Pater and others in four different books: see Nos. 71, 100, 101 and
103.

A comparison of the versions and a statement of their inter-
relationship will be found in Appendix b 3 "Wordsworth"

63   A Poet with Something to Say   23 March 1889
         [unsigned review]

         "Nights and Days" by Arthur Symons
         (London: Macmillan & Co.   1889)

         ────────────────

         Pall Mall Gazette
         Vol. XLIX   (23 March 1889), p. 3

         ────────────────

         First printed in book form in:
         UNCOLLECTED ESSAYS (1903), pp. 77-86

Published by Thomas Bird Mosher (Portland Maine, U.S.A.)
in a limited edition of 450 copies (see No. 101)

This review was also published in:
SKETCHES AND REVIEWS (1919)
Edited by Albert Mordell and published by Boni and Liveright,
New York. (see No. 103)

It should be noted that though Pater and the Pall Mall Gazette
titled the book "Nights and Days", it was really "Days and Nights".

This book was dedicated "to Walter Pater in all gratitude and
affection".

In a letter to Arthur Symons [24 March 1889] Pater writes: "I send
a line to tell you that you will find my view of "Nights and Days"
in yesterday's Pall Mall Gazette - rather hastily expressed I fear"
(see LWP No. 148)

64 Shakespere's English Kings   5 April 1889

        Scribner's Magazine
        Vol. V. (5 April 1889), pp. 506-512

        First printed in book form in:
        APPRECIATIONS (1889), pp. 192-212   (see No. 71)

In a letter dated 29 December [1888] to Arthur Symons, Pater wrote:
"I too am just completing a brief Shakespere study - The English
"Kings: - . . . " (see LWP No. 142)

A further letter to Symons [April 1889] states: "I enclose a paper,
from Scribner's Magazine, on 'Shakespere's English Kings', and
should be grateful if, at your leisure, you would point out any
thing that strikes you as behind actual Shakesperian criticism
therein, as I intend to include it in my next volume". (see LWP 149)

65 "It is Thyself"   15 April 1889
        [unsigned review]

        "It is Thyself" by Mark Raffalovich
        (London) Walter Scott: 1889

        Pall Mall Gazette
        Vol. XLIX (April 15, 1889), 3

First printed in book form in:
UNCOLLECTED ESSAYS (1903), pp. 87-92
Published by Thomas Bird Mosher (Portland, Maine, U.S.A.) in a
limited edition of 450 copies. (see No. 101)

66 "Toussaint Galabru"   April 1889

    [review]

    Toussaint Galabru by Ferdinand Fabre
    Paris: Charpentier & Cie, 1887

    ───────────────

    The Nineteenth Century
    No. CXLVI, Vol. XXV (April 1889), pp. 621-623

    ───────────────

    First printed in book form in:
    UNCOLLECTED ESSAYS (1903), pp. 93-100
    Published by Thomas Bird Mosher (Portland, Maine, U.S.A.) in a
    limited edition of 450 copies (see No. 101)

    ───────────────

This article was printed in The Nineteenth Century as part of a
series with the following heading:

    "In Feb. 1886 the Editor of The Nineteenth Century introduced a
    "new feature - NOTICEABLE BOOKS. He invited a certain number
    "of his friends to send him from time to time, in the shape of
    "letters to himself, remarks upon any books which in the
    "ordinary and natural course of their reading may strike them as
    "being worth special attention. He has suggested to them that,
    "whenever a book is thus met with - such as they would be likely
    "in the familiar conversation to advise a friend to read for
    "this or that reason - a letter should be written to the editor,
    "giving the same advice and in much the same sort of easy
    "fashion. He hopes in this way to obtain fresher and more
    "spontaneous criticism than can possibly be always produced
    "under the prevailing system of "noticing" books sent for
    "review".

This article has a special interest therefore as affording an
indication of Pater's personal predilections. It should be
remembered that he was passionately fond of France and the French
scene.   (see also No. 67: "An Idyll of the Cevennes")

67 An Idyll of the Cevennes   12 June 1889

    [unsigned review]

    Norine par Ferdinand Fabre (Paris: Charpentier)

                              35

(Paris: Charpentier)

The Guardian
No. 2256, Vol. XLIV (12 June 1889), pp. 911-912

First printed in book form in:
ESSAYS FROM THE 'GUARDIAN' (1896), pp. 115-132 as
"Ferdinand Fabre: An Idyll of the Cevennes"
Printed for Private Circulation at the Chiswick Press.
100 copies only. (see No. 100)

For a note on the Guardian see No. 39

68 Correspondance de Gustave Flaubert   3 August 1889
   Deuxième Série (1850-1854)
   (Paris: Charpentier)
   [unsigned review]

The Athenaeum
No. 3223 (3 August 1889), pp. 155-156

First printed in book form in:
UNCOLLECTED ESSAYS (1903), pp. 101-114
Published by Thomas Bird Mosher (Portland, Maine, U.S.A.) in a
limited edition of 450 copies.   (see No. 101)

Also published in:
SKETCHES AND REVIEWS (1919)
Edited by Albert Mordell, published by Boni and Liveright,
New York.   (see No. 103)

69 Hippolytus Veiled   August 1889
   A Study from Euripides

Macmillan's Magazine
No. CCCLVIII, Vol. LX (August 1889), pp. 294-306

Littell's Living Age (Boston, U.S.A.)
No. 2359, Vol. LXVII n.s., CLXXXII o.s. (14 September 1889),
   pp. 675-685

The Eclectic Magazine (New York, U.S.A.)
Vol. L, No. 4 n.s., CXIII o.s. (October 1889), pp. 507-517

First printed in book form in:
GREEK STUDIES (1895), pp. 152-186   (see No. 97)

Though this essay was included by Pater's literary executors in
GREEK STUDIES, there is reason to believe that Pater did not
consider it in such company but as part of a future volume of
Imaginary Portraits. In a letter to Arthur Symons, dated December
29th [1888] Pater wrote: "am also at work on a new portrait -
Hippolytus Veiled." In his book Figures of Several Centuries
(1916), pp. 316-333 "Walter Pater" Symons further states that
"Hippolytus Veiled was to have been an Imaginary Portrait in a
second such volume". This accords with C.L. Shadwell's Preface
to GREEK STUDIES, p. vii, in which he explains: "It was afterwards
rewritten, but with only a few substantial alterations, in Mr.
Pater's own hand, with a view, probably, of republishing it with
other essays. This last revise has been followed in the text now
printed".

Mrs Daniel, wife of Dr. C.H.O. Daniel, Provost of Worcester College,
the well-known amateur of printing, wanted to publish an article of
Pater in her husband's press. It seems that "Hippolytus Veiled"
was at first considered for this, for in an undated letter to Mrs.
Daniel, Pater writes: "I am afraid you will find 'Hippolytus'
which I send you in a revised MS copy too long; longer than I
thought. If you prefer the 'Child' I should have to revise it for
you, within the next few days". (LWP No. 265). The Child in the
House (No. 26) was in fact chosen for publication at the Daniel
Press

---

70 Giordano Bruno. Paris 1586   1 August 1889

The Fortnightly Review
No. CCLXXI, Vol. LII o.s., XLVI n.s. (1 August 1889), pp. 234-
244

Littell's Living Age (Boston, U.S.A.)
No. 2358, Vol. CLXXXII o.s., LXVII n.s. (7 September 1889),
pp. 634-640

First printed in book form in:
GASTON DE LATOUR (1896), pp. 164-200
as Chapter 7 "The Lower Pantheism"   (see No. 99)

This article was separately published by Thomas Bird Mosher
(Portland, Maine, U.S.A.) as "Giordano Bruno", Vol. XII, pp. 317
- 345, (October 1906)

In a postcard, headed Brasenose College, dated Nov. 12, to an

unknown correspondent, Pater wrote: "The article is really a
chapter from an unfinished work and had to be cut about for
insertion in the Review. This may have given it an inexplicable
air, here and there." (LWP No. 165)

From the Preface to the book, p. v, the reader will note that the
Fortnightly Review article "was afterwards largely revised and
marked Chapter VII, as it is here printed." In view of the
postcard quoted earlier however it is probable that the subsequent
book version preceded the periodical article.

The manuscript of this item is in the Berg Collection, New York
Public Library.

71 APPRECIATIONS: WITH AN ESSAY ON STYLE   15 November 1889

The Contents, in order of the book, are:

For a full description of this book, see Section I b BOOKS No. 4
APPRECIATIONS

72 Noticeable Books: 3 - A Century of Revolution   December 1889

Signed notice of:

A Century of Revolution by William Samuel Lilly
Chapman and Hall 1889

The Nineteenth Century
No. CLIV   Vol. XXVI (December 1889), pp. 992-994

First edition in book form in:
UNCOLLECTED ESSAYS (1903), pp. 115-122
Published by Thomas Bird Mosher (Portland, Maine, U.S.A.) in a
limited edition of 450 copies.   (see No. 101)

For an account of the Nineteenth Century feature "Noticeable Books"
see No. 62: "Toussaint Galabru"

We know so little of Pater's political opinions that the book
which he chose to review, dealing as it does with politics, must be
of interest.   A Century of Revolution sets out "to test the ideas
underlying the French Revolution . . . to examine the Revolution,
after a century's experience of it, in its bearing on the public
life of England."   Two quotations will indicate the genefal trend
of Lilly's comment:

> "Can we predicate freedom of the French peasant, brutalised and
> "utterly selfish, a mere human automaton, a voting animal,
> "incapable of realising his powers for the common good ?"

> "One of the latest and ugliest features of our political life
> "is the growth of a new school of Liberalism breathing the
> "spirit of the Revolutionary dogma.   Mr. Gladstone is its most
> "notable adherent.   The result . . . to sink the House of Commons
> "in ever increasing degredation."

73 IMAGINARY PORTRAITS   March 1890
        Second Edition

        CONTENTS as in the First Edition.   See No. 47

74 APPRECIATIONS: WITH AN ESSAY ON STYLE   May 1890
        Second Edition

        CONTENTS:

            As in the First Edition. See No. 71, except that
            "Aesthetic Poetry was omitted, and "Feuillet's 'La
            Morte' " was inserted between "Dante G briel Rossetti"
            and "Postcript."

75 Tales of a Hundred Years Since   16 July 1890

        [unsigned review]

        "Contes du Centenaire" Par Augustin Filon
        (Paris: Hachette et Cie)

        _____

        The Guardian
        No. 2328, Vol. XLV (16 July 1890), p. 1138

        _____

        First printed in book form in:
        ESSAYS FROM THE GUARDIAN'(1896), pp. 133-149 as
        "The 'Contes' of M. Augustin Filon: Tales of a Hundred
        Years since."
        Printed for Private Circulation at the Chiswick Press.
        100 copies only.   (see No. 100)

        For the Guardian articles see note on No. 39

76 "On Viol and Flute"   29 October 1890
        by Edmund Gosse (Kegan Paul)

        [unsigned review]

        _____

        The Guardian
        No. 2343, Vol. XLV (29 October 1890), pp. 1712-1713

        _____

        First printed in book form in:
        ESSAYS FROM THE 'GUARDIAN' (1896), pp. 149-163
        as "Mr. Gosses's Poems"
        Printed for Private Circulation at the Chiswick Press.
        100 copies only.   (see No. 100)

        For the Guardian articles see note on No. 39

        _____

Edward William Gosse (1849-1928) - knighted in 1925 - was a firm
friend of Walter Pater and his sisters, and contributed the article
on "WALTER HORATIO PATER" to the Dictionary of National Biography.
Though they were good friends Pater's mind eluded Gosse, and it is
doubtful if they were really intimate.   Many of the facts and
anecdotes now known to us of Pater's life at Oxford and London come
from Gosse.

A number of letters from Pater to Gosse are in the Brotherton
Collection, University of Leeds..   Biographers will find The Book
of Gosse, now in the Cambridge University Library, of great interes

One other tenuous link: in 1929 E.H. Blakeney printed Two
Unpublished Poems by Gosse.   In the previous year he had published
two poems by Pater (see Nos. 1 and 2)

77 Art Notes in North Italy   (written) October 1890

The New Review
No. XVIII, Vol. III (November 1890), pp. 393-403

Littell's Living Age (Boston: U.S.A.)
No. 2423, Vol. LXXII n.s., CLXXXVII o.s. (6 December 1890)
   pp. 625-630

First printed in book form in:
MISCELLANEOUS STUDIES (1895), pp. 85-104   (see No. 98)

In a letter to Arthur Symons, dated Oct. 18th [1890], Pater wrote:
"I never got to Italy after all, this summer: instead, finished a
paper of Art-Notes in North Italy, by way of prologue to an
Imaginary Portrait with Brescia for background. The former will,
I think, appear shortly, in one of the monthlies." (See LWP No. 189
The editor Mr. Lawrence Evans states that "The 'Imaginary Portrait
with Brescia for background' is the unpublished MS fragment,
'Gaudioso, the Second,' now at Harvard.")

78 Prosper Merimee   December 1890

The Fortnightly Review
No. CCLXXXVII, Vol. LIV o.s., XLVIII n.s. (December 1890), pp.
   852-864

Littell's Living Age (Boston: U.S.A.)
No. 2429, Vol. LXXIII n.s., CLXXXVIII o.s. (17 January 1891),
   pp. 131-139

First printed in book form in:
MISCELLANEOUS STUDIES (1895), pp. 1-29   (see No. 98)

Also published in:
Studies in European Literature: Being the Taylorian Lectures
1889-1899 (Oxford: The Clarendon Press), 1900. pp. 31-54
A foundation was made for an Annual Lecture at the Taylor
Institution on some subject of Foreign Literature. Provision
was made for the publication of the lectures and this volume
contained those so far delivered. The eleven lectures in this
volume were given by: Professor Down, Walter H. Pater, W.M.
Rossetti, T.W. Rolleston, Stephen Mallarme, A. Morel-Fatio,
H.R. Brown, Paul Bourget, Professor Herford, Henry Butler
Clarke and Professor Ker.

"Prosper Merimee" was given as a lecture at the Taylor Institute,
Oxford, on 17th November 1890, and at the London Institute, 24th
November 1890

[review]

"The Picture of Dorian Gray" by Oscar Wilde
(Ward, Lock and Co. London, New York and Melbourne)

The Bookman
Vol. I (November 1891), pp. 59-60

First printed in book form in:
UNCOLLECTED ESSAYS (1893), pp. 123-134
Published by Thomas Bird Mosher (Portland, Maine, U.S.A.) in a
limited editon of 450 copies   (see No. 101)

Also published in:
SKETCHES AND REVIEWS (1919)
Edited by Albert Mordell.   Published by Boni and Liveright, New
York.   (see No. 103)

Thomas Wright in The Life of Walter Pater (1907) states in Vol. II,
pages 156-159 that "Wilde submitted it [the manuscript of Dorian
Gray] to Pater who, though he seems to have taken no particular
interest in it, suggested some alterations in the phraseology, which
were carried out; and in due time it went to press."

Alfred Douglas wrote the following letter to the Times Literary
Supplement (Aug. 12, 1939, p. 479):

"Sir, - The Writer in the Times Literary Supplement last week of
"an article on Walter Pater's centenary would have been well
"advised if, before indulging in a cheap sneer at Oscar Wilde's
"enthralling story "The Picture of Dorian Gray" (whose author he
"compared to Martin Tupper), he had recalled the fact that Walter
"Pater himself was not only a great friend of Oscar Wilde's, but
"that he reviewed "The Picture of Dorian Gray" in the Bookman at
"the time of its publication in London, and gave it the highest
"praise.   If your contributor really has such a great opinion
"of Walter Pater as he professes it is surprising that he should
"neglect to correct his own judgment by that of his master. The
"sneer at Wilde and his masterpiece would have caused Walter
"Pater the greatest indignation and resentment. The unfairness
"and rancour of the Press which pursued Oscar Wilde all through
"his life might surely, one had hoped, be allowed to die down
"forty years after his death. "

The Contemporary Review

No. LXI (February 1892), 249-261

Littell's Living Age (Boston: U.S.A.)
No. 2493, Vol. LXXVIII n.s. CXC III o.s. (9 April 1892), pp.
67-74

The Eclectic Magazine (N.Y., U.S.A.)
No. 4, Vol. LV n.s., CXVIII o.s., (April 1892), pp. 454-462

First printed in book form in:
PLATO AND PLATONISM: A SERIES OF LECTURES (1893), pp. 112-135
as Chapter VI, with the same title   (see No. 87)

"The Genius of Plato" was one of a series of lectures given by Pater
at Brasenose College, Oxford, 1891-1892.   For a note on Pater as a
lecturer see Appendix b 1

Pater wrote the following letter to Percy William Bunting, editor of
the Contemporary Review: December 21 [1891]

"I send you, by this post, a MS on 'The Genius of Plato', which
"I hope you may find suitable for the Contemporary Review. I
"have treated the subject in as popular a manner as I could.
"If you care to have it, I should like it to appear in the Feb-
"ruary number. I have no other complete copy of the MS.
(see LWP. No. 208)

81 A Chapter on Plato   (written) January 1892

Macmillan's Magazine
No. CCCXCI, Vol. LXVI (May 1892), pp. 31-38

Littell's Living Age (Boston: U.S.A.)
No. 2503, Vol. LXXVIII n.s., CXCIII o.s. (18 June 1892), pp. 762-
763

The Eclectic Magazine (N.Y., U.S.A.)
No. 1 Vol. LVI n.s., CXIX o.s. (July 1892), pp. 63-72

First printed in book form in:
PLATO AND PLATONISM; A SERIES OF LECTURES (1893), pp. 1-20,
as Chapter I "Plato and the Doctrine of Motion." (See No. 87)

"A Chapter on Plato" was one of a series of lectures given by Pater
at Brasenose College, Oxford, 1891-1892.   For a note on Pater as a
lecturer see Appendix c 1

The Contemporary Review
Vol. LXI (June 1892), 790-808

Littell's Living Age (Boston)
No. 2509, Vol. LXXIX n.s., CXCIV o.s. (30 July 1892), pp. 284-294

The Eclectic Magazine (N.Y., U.S.A.)
No. 2, Vol. LVI n.s., CXIX o.s. (August 1892), pp. 145-157

First printed in book form in:
PLATO AND PLATONISM: A SERIES OF LECTURES (1893), pp. 179-213
as Chapter VIII under the same title   (see No. 87)

Letter from Pater to William Canton, assistant editor of the
Contemporary Review, dated May 17th [1892]:

   "I enclose the corrected proof of my paper on 'Lacedaemon".
   "I found that, like my last paper, it greatly needed
   "subdivision into paragraphs.   I suppose this is due to the
   "circumstance that it was written for delivery as a lecture.
   "I have done the best I could to subdivide it"
   (see LWP No. 219)

83 Emerald Uthwart   June & July 1892

The New Review
Vol. VI (June 1892), pp. 708-722
    VII (July 1892),   42- 54

First printed in book form in:
MISCELLANEOUS STUDIES (1895), pp. 198-250   (see No. 98)

This piece was published as a separate volume as
EMERALD UTHWART: AN IMAGINARY PORTRAIT (July 1899) by Thomas
Bird Mosher (Portland, Maine, U.S.A.) in his 'Brocade' series,
XV,84 pages, Japan Vellum.   It was a limited edition of 425
copies, printed at the press of George D. Loring, Portland.
A second edition was published in June 1900

EMERALD UTHWART was also published in a privately printed
edition by Pater's old school, Kings, Canterbury (1905).   48 pp
bound in dark blue cloth;   lettered "Emerald Uthwart" in gold o
spine and front cover;   College coat of arms in gold on front
cover.

M.dHangest, in his Walter Pater: l'homme et l'oeuvre (Paris:

THE
PURGATORY
OF
DANTE ALIGHIERI

(PURGATORIO I–XXVII)

AN EXPERIMENT IN
LITERAL VERSE TRANSLATION

BY

CHARLES LANCELOT SHADWELL, M.A., B.C.L.
FELLOW OF ORIEL COLLEGE, OXFORD

WITH AN INTRODUCTION

BY

WALTER PATER, M.A.
FELLOW OF BRASENOSE COLLEGE, OXFORD.

LONDON
MACMILLAN AND CO.
AND NEW YORK
1892

1961), says (Vol. II p. 324) that "Emerald Uthwart" was
inspired by a visit made by Pater to his old school in the
summer of 1891.

84   MARIUS THE EPICUREAN :   10 August 1892
     HIS SENSATIONS AND IDEAS   2 vols.

     Third edition

     _____

For a full description of this edition, see Section I b BOOKS:
No. 2 MARIUS THE EPICUREAN

85   Introduction to   (Prior to) 9 September 1892

     The Purgatory of Dante Alighieri (Purgatorio I-XXVII)
     translated by Charles Lancelot Shadwell
     (Macmillan and Co. 1892)

     _____

     The Preface by Shadwell is dated 9 September 1892

     This introduction is included in:
     UNCOLLECTED ESSAYS (1903), pp. 143-161, as
     "Shadwell's Dante"
     Published by Thomas Bird Mosher (Portland, Maine, U.S.A.) in a
     limited edition of 450 copies   (see No. 101)

     _____

Charles Lancelot Shadwell, Provost of Oriel, was a close friend of
Pater.   He later acted as Pater's literary executor.

The Introduction by Pater takes pp. xiii-xxviii, the text pp. 2-
411, with text and translation on opposite pages.

The University of Michigan have in their Rare Book Department of
the University Library a copy of:

     Dante Alighieri. La Vita nuova e il canzoniere . . .
     Commenteti de G.R. Giuliani.   Firenze, G. Burbera, editors
     1863.
     Autographed on fly-leaf: "Walter Pater"

86   Raphael   October 1892

     _____

     The Fortnightly Review
     No. CCVII, Vol. LVIII o.s., LII n.s. (October 1892), pp.
        458-469

Littell's Living Age (Boston, U.S.A.)
No. 2528, Vol. LXXX n.s., CXCV o.s. (10 December 1892), pp. 645-691

First printed in book form in:
MISCELLANEOUS STUDIES (1895), pp. 30-54 (see No. 98)

87 PLATO AND PLATONISM: A SERIES OF LECTURES   9 February 1893

CONTENTS:
    Chapter   I   Plato and the Doctrine of Motion   See No. 81
             II   Plato and the Doctrine of Rest
          III Plato and the Doctrine of Number
          IV Plato and Socrates
           V Plato and the Sophists
          VI The Genius of Plato   See No. 80
         VII The Doctrine of Plato
                 1. The Theory of Ideas
                 2. Dialectic
       VIII Lacedaemon   See No. 82
          IX The Republic
           X Plato's Aesthetics

For a full description of this book and its contents, see Section I b. No. 5 PLATO AND PLATONISM

These lectures were delivered to students at Brasenose College in the years 1891-1892

The Bodleian Library, Oxford own the manuscript of Pater's essay on "Pascal" (see No. 96). Part of the manuscript is backed by the draft of an essay on "Plato's Republic" (verso of pages 14, 15, 18-21, 25-30, 32-33)

88. Mr. George Moore as an Art Critic   10 June 1893
    [Review]

    "Modern Painting" by George Moore
    (London: Walter Scott 1893)

Daily Chronicle
10 June 1893

First printed in book form in:
UNCOLLECTED ESSAYS (1903), pp. 135-142
Published by Thomas Bird Mosher (Portland, Maine, U.S.A.) in a
limited edition of 450 copies   (see No. 101)

Also published in
SKETCHES AND REVIEWS (1919)   (see No. 103)
Edited by Albert Mordell and published by Boni and Liveright,
New York

89 The Age of Athletic Prizemen: (written) prior to 7 November 1893
    A Chapter in Greek Art

The Contemporary Review
Vol. LXV (February 1894), pp. 242-256

First Printed in book form in:
GREEK STUDIES (1895), pp. 283-315   (see No. 97)

In a letter dated Nov. 7th [1893] to William Canton, Assistant
Editor of the Contemporary Review, Pater wrote: "I send to your
address by this post a MS. for the Contemporary Review." The MS.
was "The Age of Athletic Prizemen: A Chapter in Greek Art"

90 Apollo in Picardy   November 1893

Harper's New Monthly Magazine
Vol. XXVI European edition; Vol. LXXXVII American edition. Both
November 1893. pp. 949-957 in the European edition.

Note: Harper's Magazine is still in existence

The European and American editions were the same in content and
general format, but the English edition carried English
advertising.

The editor has no records which would explain why Pater published
this one article in Harper's. He suggests that Pater was
invited by the then Editor to provide an essay, and was offered
a good price for it. In those days Harper's were paying very
high prices in comparison with most other magazines.

The manuscript is not on their files.

First printed in book form in:
MISCELLANEOUS STUDIES (1895), pp. 140-170 (see No. 98)

M.d'Hangest in his Walter Pater: l'homme et l'oeuvre (Paris: 1961)
writes: "Pater se proposait de l'inclure dans une deuxième serie
de Portraits imaginaires que sa mort l'empêche de compléter." II.324-
M. d'Hangest may have taken this information from Arthur Symons's
Figures of Several Centuries (1916), in which interesting
information is given on Pater's projects in 1889 for further
Imaginary Portraits.

T. Wright, Life of Walter Pater, Vol. II, p. 197, also states that
at this time Pater was intent "on a series of sketches, chiefly on
subjects relating to Greek thought and mythology, which were to form
a second series of Imaginary Portraits. The only sketch finished,
however, was that suggested by Domenichino's picture, namely,
'Apollo in Picardy', which appeared in Harper's Magazine in the
November of that year (1893)."

91   THE RENAISSANCE: STUDIES IN ART AND POETRY   December 1893
       Fourth edition of
       STUDIES IN THE HISTORY OF THE RENAISSANCE   (see No. 16)

     The CONTENTS are as in the Third edition   (see No. 51)

92   Some Great Churches in France   (written) January 1894
         1. Notre-Dame D'Amiens

     The Nineteenth Century
     No. XXV, Vol. XXXV (March 1894), pp. 481-488

     Littell's Living Age (Boston: U.S.A.)
     No. 2595, Vol. I - 6th s., CC o.s. (31 March 1894), pp. 792-797

     First printed in book form in:
     MISCELLANEOUS STUDIES (1895), pp. 105-122, as
     "Notre-Dame d'Amiens"

     This essay also appeared, together with No. 94, in:
     Some Great Churches in France
     Three essays by William Morris and Walter Pater, published by
     Thomas Bird Mosher, in his 'Brocade' series, XXXIX, (1903), a
     limited edition of 425 copies. The volume was printed on Japan
     vellum, by George D. Loring, Portland, Maine, and was of 108
     pages.

A second edition was published in December 1905 and a third in
November 1912
The Morris essay was "Shadow of Amiens"

A letter from Pater to James Thomas Knowles, editor of the
Nineteenth Century, helps to date this essay: Jan. 22nd [1894]

> "I send you, by this post, a short paper on Notre-Dame
> "d'Amiens, which I think you may find suitable for the
> "Nineteenth Century.   It is first of a series, to be
> "ready at intervals, on 'Some Great Churches of France',
> "but it might appear without the general title". (LWP. 255)

There is some evidence that when Pater was a schoolboy he was
greatly interested in Church architecture and well informed on it.
This is stated in a letter, dated 26th March 1904, from his old
school friend, John Rainier McQueen, to Thomas Wright, the
biographer of Pater (ms. University of Indiana):

> "Pater was always fond of Church architecture, and knew a
> "great deal about it, when quite a lad. Almost the first
> "time I visited him at Harbledown, he took me into the old
> "Church of the Hospital (or Almshouses) there, and pointed
> "out its architectural characteristics. I think this taste
> "must have remained with him throughout."

93 Mr. F.W. Bussell   (written) March 1894

Published in:
Oxford Characters
A Series of Lithographs
by Will Rothenstein (1896), Part VI

Oxford Characters was a collection of lithographs of notable Oxford
personalities, published by John Lane.   Part I appeared in June
1893, Part Vi separately in 1896.

The Sketch of Bussell was made in 1894 when he was thirty-two years
of age.   Pater introduced Rothenstein and Bussell.   Bussell was
the most intimate friend of Pater's later years, and Part VI
contained their two lithographs.   Pater wrote the description
which prefaces the sketch.   As the lines are rarely available, I
give them below:

Mr. F.W. Bussell

Fellow of B.N.C.,   B.D.,   and Mus. Bac.

Is as young as he looks here.   He was early distinguished
in the University and has already preached some
remarkable sermons in Saint Mary's pulpit.   His friends

love him: and he is popular with the undergraduates
whom he instructs. His versatility is considerable:
but he is above all a student, with something like
genius for classical literature, especially early
Christian theology and late Pagan philosophy of the
imperial age, which he reads as other people read the
newspapers. His expression after hours of such
reading is here recorded with remarkable firmness. He
is capable of much.

WALTER PATER

In a letter to Will Rothenstein, dated March 11th [1894] Pater

wrote: "I think your likeness of Bussell most excellent and shall

value it." (LWP No. 260)

The Rev.Frederick William Bussell (1862-1944) was the greatest friend
of Pater's later years. His funeral oration on Pater, which
contains many interesting personal details, will be found in
Appendix 3 c
He was a versatile scholar, who occupied many clerical and
University posts. Author of numerous publications, mainly
concerned with Theology, Classical History (he shared Pater's
interest in Marcus Aurelius) and Constitution. He was a composer
of merit for voices, strings and organ. He lectured in the
Classics, Philosophy, Theology and Modern History.

An unknown anecdote: Pater and Bussell often entertained students
to dinner, each sitting at one end of a long table, with the young
men on either side. Halfway through the course of the meal, each
would stand up and exchange seats in order that they could talk
to all present. (Told to me by one of the young men).

94 Some Great Churches in France   (written) May 1894
        2. Vezelay

The Nineteenth Century
Vol. XXXV (June 1894), pp. 963-970

Littell's Living Age (Boston: U.S.A.)
No. 2611, Vol. III 6th s., CCII o.s. 21 July 1894)

First printed in book form in:
MISCELLANEOUS STUDIES (1895), pp. 123-139, as
"Vezelay"

This essay, together with No. 92, also appeared in:
Some Great Churches in France   (see No. 92 "Notre-Dame d'Amiens
for details.

This essay has been translated into French:

VÉZELAY: Essai d'histoire d'art religeux. Traduit
de l'anglais par Dr. L. Vignes, Avallon. imp de la
Revue de l'yonne (1914), 8vo. 15 pp.

95 AN IMAGINARY PORTRAIT   June 1894

        Printed by H. Daniel at his Private Press
        at Oxford in a limited edition of 250 copies

                    _____

        This portrait first appeared as:
        "Imaginary Portraits
            1. The Child in the House"

        in:
        Macmillan's Magazine
        Vol. XXXVIII No. CCXXVI (August 1878), pp. 313-321. (see No. 27)

        For a complete description of this book and the circumstances of
        publication, see Section I b BOOKS No. 6 AN IMAGINARY PORTRAIT

                    _____

When preparing this essay for Provost Daniel, Pater took an offset of
the Macmillan's Magazine article and revised it. This offset/
manuscript is at Worcester College Library, Oxford.

POSTHUMOUS   PUBLICATIONS

The Contemporary Review
Vol. LXVII (February 1895), pp. 168-181

First printed in book form in:
MISCELLANEOUS STUDIES (1895), pp. 55-84   (see No. 98)

The article when printed in the Contemporary Review was prefaced as
follows: "The following study of Pascal is the latest of the works
of Mr. Pater. He was still engaged upon it at the time of his
death, and had not, as will be observed, entirely finished it.
There is, however, reason to believe that he would not have greatly
extended it. It is printed here, with as close adherence to his
text as possible, from his scored and tormented original MS. All
who were acquainted with Mr. Pater's critical work will be glad to
receive this last contribution to it, although it lacks the polish
of his final revision."

M. d'Hangest in his Walter Pater: l'homme et l'oeuvre (Paris: 1961)
writes: "Étude inachevée, ecrite pour une conference qui serait
être faite en juillet 1894 a Oxford."

The MS of this essay is in the Bodleian Library, Oxford. It
consists of 83 pages in quarto plus a large number of slips of paper
It is accompanied by a note of Sir Edmund Gosse and two letters of
Clara Pater, who offered it to him after the publication of the text
in MISCELLANEOUS STUDIES

It appears that Edmund Gosse offered to purchase the MS of Pascal.
He had prepared the essay for the Contemporary Review printing and
wished to own it. On June 25th 1895 Clara Pater wrote a charming
letter to him in which she said:

"We could not possibly part with the Pascal manuscript for money
"It is the last thing Walter wrote & was writing even during his
"illness, & so is precious to us. But as we know your friend-
"ship for him, & are sure you would value & cherish it, you
"shall have it bye and bye as a gift. It will be wanted by Mr.
"Shadwell in bringing out the next volume of Essays, as he would
"naturally like to make his own emendations from the original
"M.S. rather than from the printed article - But after that, all
"the M.S.S. will be returned to us, & we will hand that one to
"you . . . " (LWP No. 271)

Later in the year, Nov. 13, 1895, Clara wrote to Gosse:

"I am just sending off the "Pascal" manuscript, which please
"accept with many thanks for all the trouble you took with it.
"It has been very much praised in one of the papers, so I am
"glad we published it, in spite of its incompleteness . . . "

The following note is with the M.S. at the Bodleian Library:

"This box contains the original MS. of Walter Pater's last
"composition, the "Pascal", on which he was engaged when he was

"taken ill, in June 1894. The last sentences, the latest he
"wrote, were put on paper not many days before he died, July 30
"1894. This MS. was given to me to be disciplined, and from
"my collation it was published in the "Contemporary Review".
"After publication of the "Miscellaneous Studies" it was
"presented to me by Miss Hester and Miss Clara Pater. The
"letter with which the latter accompanied the gift is also here,
"together with a rare early portrait of the author."

E.G.

January 1896

When the MS was bought by Friends of the Bodleian at the Woodward
sale, 23 January 1945, no portrait was found.

In English Literature: An Illustrated Record, by Edmund Gosse, Vol
IV (Heinemann: 1903) will be found a facsimile page of Pater's
'Pascal', together with an attractive photograph.

Doubts have been cast on Gosse's rendering of the manuscript, and
another version would be welcome.

97 GREEK STUDIES: A SERIES OF ESSAYS   11 January 1895

CONTENTS, in order of the book:

A Study of Dionysus: The Spiritual Form of Fire and Dew	See No. 22
The Bacchanals of Euripides	25
The Myth of Demeter and Persephone	20
Hippolytus Veiled: A Study from Euripides	69
The Beginnings of Greek Sculpture.	
1. The Heroic Age of Greek Art	30
II. The Age of Graven Images	30
The Marbles of Aegina	31
The Age of Athletic Prizemen A Chapter in Greek Art	89

For a description of this book and contents, together with
circumstances of composition, see Section I b BOOKS, No. 7 -
GREEK STUDIES (1895)

98 MISCELLANEOUS STUDIES: A SERIES OF ESSAYS   11 October 1895

CONTENTS, in order of the book:

For a full description of this book and its contents, together with
circumstances of composition, see Section I b BOOKS No. 8 -
MISCELLANEOUS STUDIES (1895)

99 GASTON DE LATOUR: AN UNFINISHED ROMANCE   6 October 1896

CONTENTS:

For Chapters I - V: See Nos 51-55 of this section

           VI was taken from papers found after Pater's
                  death

          VII See No. 69: "Giordano Bruno"

For a description of this book and its contents, together with
circumstances of composition, see Section I b BOOKS No. 9 -
GASTON DE LATOUR (1896)

100   ESSAYS FROM THE "GUARDIAN"   1896

Printed for Private Circulation at the
Chiswick Press. 100 copies only.

CONTENTS in order of the book:

For a description of this book and its contents, together with
circumstances of publication, see Section I b BOOKS: No. 10 –
ESSAYS FROM THE "GUARDIAN" (1896)

101   UNCOLLECTED ESSAYS BY WALTER PATER   1903

Published by Thomas Bird Mosher, Portland, Maine, U.S.A.,
in a limited edition of 450 copies

CONTENTS in order of the book:

For a description of this book and its contents, see Section I b
BOOKS: No. 11 UNCOLLECTED ESSAYS (1903)

A note on Thomas Bird Mosher will be found in Appendix a.
"Thomas Bird Mosher: Man of Letters"

102 COLERIDGE'S WRITINGS   1910

This was published as a small $3\frac{1}{2}$" x $5\frac{3}{4}$" book by Gowans and Gray,
London and Glasgow in 1910, as No. 40 of Gowans International
Library. It is a paper back book of 48 pages, priced 6d.

An introductory note states: "As none of Walter Pater's works
have been reprinted in this country in a really cheap form, it
is hoped that the present booklet will be appreciated by many.
The essay it contains was first published in the Westminster
Review for January 1866, and afterwards reprinted in the volume
called APPRECIATIONS"

This essay is here listed as it is the first printing in book form
of the Westminster Review article in its entirety. The APPRECIATIONS
version was not complete.

See No. 4 for details of the Review printing and other information on
the essay.

103 SKETCHES AND REVIEWS   1919

Published by Boni and Liveright: New York
Edited by Albert Mordell

CONTENTS in order of the book:

1. Aesthetic Poetry   See No. 6

2. M. Lemaitre's "Serenus and other Tales"   50

3. The Life and Letters of Gustave
        Flaubert   59

4. "Correspondance of Gustave Flaubert"   68

5. Coleridge as a Theologian   4

6. Wordsworth   61

7. A Novel by Mr. Oscar Wilde   79

8. A Poet with Something to say   63

9. Mr. George Moore as an Art Critic   88

For a description of this book and its contents, with circumstances of publication, see Section I b BOOKS: No.   12 <u>SKETCHES AND REVIEWS</u> (1919)

PUBLISHED WRITINGS

b. BIBLIOGRAPHICAL RECORD OF ALL BOOKS, INCLUDING
COLLECTED AND SELECTED EDITIONS

NOTE: The individual books, Nos. 1 - 14 below have been listed
in Section I a : "Chronological Record of all periodical
and book publications" but are given here with detail and
comment.

I have included all books published in Pater's lifetime
and others which might be held to have some first edition
value.

1.   STUDIES IN THE HISTORY OF THE RENAISSANCE

a. First edition   1873

Title-page:
    STUDIES/ IN THE HISTORY OF THE/ RENAISSANCE/ by/ WALTER H. PATER/
    Fellow of Brasenose College, Oxford/ London [Gothic type]/ MACMILLAN
    AND CO./ 1873/ [All rights reserved]

Imprint:
    p. [214] OXFORD:/ By T. Combe, M.A., E.B. Gardiner, E. Pickard
    Hall, and J.H. Stacy,/ PRINTERS TO THE UNIVERSITY.

Format:
    Extra crown octavo: 7 7/8" x 5¼"

Signatures:
    [A]^8 B - O^8 P^4

Pagination:
    [i - vii]   viii - xiv   [xv - xvi]   [1] 2 - 213 [214 - 210]

Contents:
    p. [i] half-title: STUDIES/ IN THE HISTORY OF THE/ RENAISSANCE;
    [ii] Publisher's circular device: MM, butterflies, stars and
    acorns; [iii] title-page [see above]; [iv] blank; [v] dedica-
    tion: TO/ C.L.S. ; [vi] blank; [vii] viii-xiv Preface; [xv]
    Contents; [xvi] blank; [1] 2-213 text; [214] imprint [see
    above]; [215-216] advertisements: Macmillan and Co.'s Publications

    The "C.L.S." of the dedication was Pater's friend Charles Lancelot
    Shadwell, who arranged for the publication of several posthumous
    works.

Binding:
    Dark green cloth, lettered in gold across spine: STUDIES/ IN THE
    HISTORY/ OF THE/ RENAISSANCE/ [short rule]/ W.H.PATER/ [double rule]

    See John Carter, Binding Variants in English Publishing: 1820-1900
    (Constable & Co. Ltd., 1932), p. 145. Two variants are given: "A.
    The Words OF THE in the title on the spine are 9 mm. long and the
    rule 10 mm. long.   B. OF THE measures 15 mm. and the rule 8 mm.
    This is a very small difference between two otherwise identical
    bindings, and it may have no significance.   It should be recorded,
    however, that Macmillan's file copy is in A. as is the British
    Museum copy (Received April 2, 1873)"

    Chocolate end papers.

    The paper used in this edition was specially made "to imitate the
    old fashioned paper" and its "mock rib" pleased the publisher and
    Pater very much.

Number published and price:
    1250 at 7s. 6d.

Date of Publication:
    15th February 1873

STUDIES

IN THE HISTORY OF THE

RENAISSANCE

BY

WALTER H. PATER

FELLOW OF BRASENOSE COLLEGE, OXFORD

London

MACMILLAN AND CO.

1873

CONTENTS:

The book contained the following papers.   The periodical and date
of prior printing, if any, are placed after the title, and reference is
made to the Chronological RECORD in Section I a :

A comparison of the four versions of this review
which were prepared by Pater will be found in
Appendix b 2: "Conclusion"

CIRCUMSTANCES OF PUBLICATION

We are fortunate in having direct evidence of the negotiations
between Pater and Alexander Macmillan which lead to the publication of
STUDIES IN THE HISTORY OF THE RENAISSANCE. One interesting source is
the centenary volume The House of Macmillan 1843-1943 by Charles Morgan
(1943).   In 1964-65 Macmillan and Co. decided to place their pre-1939
letter books containing some 130,000 copy letters, together with their
correspondence files in the custody of the British Museum (see Letters
to Macmillan selected and edited by Simon Nowell-Smith, 1967).   These
letter books and correspondence were exhaustively examined by Dr.
Lawrence G. Evans whose book Letters of Walter Pater (LWP) was published
by the Oxford University Press in 1970.

The publication was preceded by an amiable struggle between Pater and Alexander Macmillan. Pater, courteous in his old-fashioned rather old-maidish manner, but persistent; Macmillan handling his difficult client with an admirable mixture of patience, kindness, yet magisterial authority.

As stated by Charles Morgan, the first approach seems to have come from Pater, who called on Macmillan and then on June 29th, 1872 wrote: "I send you by this post the papers of which I spoke" (LWP No. 12). At that moment the proposal was to publish four essays which had appeared in the Fortnightly Review ("Notes on Leonardo da Vinci", "A fragment on Sandro Botticelli", "Pico della Mirandula" and "The Poetry of Michelangelo") ; the essay on Winckelmann which had been printed in the Westminster Review; and other papers, only one of which had been as yet completed.

Alexander Macmillan accepted the book promptly, proposing an octavo volume. Then ensued an amusing, polite but stubborn battle between author and publisher. Pater evidently wanted his book to be artistic in appearance and not to be bound in the normal cloth. On Nov. 2nd 1872 he proposed a small volume "in paste-board with paper back and printed title . . . It would, I am sure, be much approved of by many persons of taste, among whom the sale of the book would probably in the first instance be". (LWP No. 14) He proposed covers of a greyish blue a paper back of olive green "nothing could be prettier or more simple". He also yearned for "paper with rough edges and showing the water-mark".

Macmillan proved obdurate: "my experience leads me to think that an 8vo. volume is most suitable for a book as yours" (7 Nov. 1872). Pater battled on: "Something not quite in the ordinary way is, I must repeat, very necessary in a volume the contents of which are so unpretending as mine, and which is intended in the first instance for a comparatively small section of readers. For a book on art to be bound in the ordinary way is, it seems to me, behind the times; and the difficulty of getting a book in cloth so as to be at all artistic and indeed not quite the other way, is very great". (Nov. 11th, 1872: LWP No. 15)

However, the publisher insisted in imposing his authority. In the end Pater capitulated, writing on Nov 13 1872: "The volume you send seems to me a beautiful specimen of printing, and I should much like to have the same sort of paper. I like the black cover, and think, with some modifications, about which I will write shortly, it will do very well for my book". (LWP No. 16)

The agreement for the publication of this book was dated 4th January 1873. Information regarding the details of Victorian publishing is not plentiful and it may be of interest to quote the agreement for this famous book:

"IT IS AGREED that the said Messrs Macmillan and Co.
"shall publish at their own expense and risk.

Studies in the History of the Renaissance
and after deducting from the produce of the sale
thereof, all the expenses of printing, paper, boarding,
advertising and incidental expenses, the profits
remaining of every edition which may be printed of the

work during the legal term of Copyright, are to be
divided into two equal parts, one moiety to be paid
to the said Walter H. Pater, Esq., and the other
moiety to belong to Messrs Macmillan & Co.

The books to be accounted for at the Trade-Sale Price,
twenty-five as Twenty-four, unless it be thought
advisable to dispose of copies, or of the remainder at
a lower price, which is left to the judgment and
discretion of Messrs Macmillan and Co.

Accounts to be made up annually to Midsummer, and
delivered on or before October 1 and settled by cash
in the ensuing January."

At this point it may be as well to state that Pater never considered
changing his publisher and had the warmest possible feeling towards him.
Indeed, while arranging for a second edition of The Renaissance,he wrote
to Alexander Macmillan on September 14th, 1876: "I am not one of those
(if such there be) who complain of the useful office of the Publishers;
and I know not how long ago I formed the ambition that you should
publish what I might write as I gleaned over the fascinating list of
your publications in the "higher" literature - certainly before I
could afford to buy them."

The book was retitled:

THE RENAISSANCE: STUDIES IN ART AND POETRY

The change of title followed upon criticism of the title and
scope of the book as first published. In particular, Mrs Mark
Pattison when reviewing, patronisingly, the book in the <u>Westminster
Review</u>, Vol. XLIII n.s. (April 1873), pp. 639-641, wrote: "The
title is misleading. The Historical element is precisely that
which is wanting, and its absence makes the weak place of the whole
book . . . But the work is in no wise a contribution to the history
of the Renaissance".

<u>Title-page:</u>
THE RENAISSANCE/ <u>STUDIES IN ART AND POETRY</u>/ by/ WALTER PATER/
Fellow of Brasenose College, Oxford/ <u>second edition, revised</u>/
[vignette in red]/ LONDON/ MACMILLAN AND CO./ 1877/ [All rights
reserved]

<u>Imprint:</u>
p. [226] OXFORD:/ by E. Pickard Hall, M.A., and J.H. Stacy,/
Printers to the University.

<u>Format:</u>
Extra crown octavo: 8" x 5 3/8"

<u>Signatures:</u>
[a]2 b^8 B - P^8 Q^2

<u>Pagination:</u>
[i - vii]   viii - xv   [xvi - xx]   [1] 2 - 225 [226-228]

<u>Contents:</u>
p. [i] half-title: THE RENAISSANCE; [ii] blank; [tissue guard];
[iii] title-page [see above]; [iv] blank; [v] dedication: To/
C.L.S. [in black letter]; [vi] blank; [vii] viii-xv Preface; [xvi]
blank; [xvii] contents; [xviii] blank; [xix] fly-title: THE
RENAISSANCE; [xx] blank; [1] 2-225 text; [226] imprint [see
above]; [227-228] Publisher's advertisements: Works on Art

<u>Binding:</u>
Dark-blue cloth, lettered in gold across spine: The/ RENAISSANCE/
WALTER/ PATER/ MACMILLAN/ AND CO.

<u>Number published and price:</u>
1,250 at 10s. 6d.

Date of Publication:
24th May 1877
<u>American edition:</u> [January] 1887 [1000] copies

    An interesting feature of the title-page for the second edition was
the vignette, later described by Macmillan's as 'after Leonardo da Vinci'
It had been engraved by Charles Henry Jeans (1827-1879), a well-known
British artist. Some of his earliest independent employment was on
postage-stamps for the English colonies. About 1860 he became
associated with Messrs Macmillan & Co. and produced many beautiful
vignettes and portraits for their 'Golden Treasury' and other series. A
volume of proofs of his vignettes is in the print room of the British

Museum.

See later comment for the subject of the vignette and Pater's opinion
of the engraving.

CONTENTS:

This edition contained the following papers. Reference is made to
the Chronological RECORD in Section I a :

There are certain points of difference between this edition and the
first (1873) one:

1. Change of title - see above

2. Vignette on title-page - see above

3. "Aucassin and Nicolette" was expanded to include a thirteenth-
   century "Li Amitiez de Ami et Amile" and given the title of
   "Two Early French Stories"

4. "Pico della Mirandula" became "Pico della Mirandola"

5. "Lionardo da Vinci" became "Leonardo da Vinci"

6. "Conclusion" was omitted from this edition, without comment.
   See the third edition for Pater's reason for this.   For my
   surmise on the background to the omission, see Appendix b 2

CIRCUMSTANCES OF PUBLICATION

In respect of this edition we are again fortunate in being able to
draw on a number of letters between Pater and Macmillan & Co.
Alexander Macmillan proposed a second edition as early as November 1876,
and Pater gladly accepted, though he showed ominous signs of wanting to
dictate the format of the book when he added "I should like the new
edition to be as perfect as possible."   He added he wouldlike to
include an engraved vignette.   This is the one after Leonardo da
Vinci which was printed as he proposed.   In the same letter (Nov. 15 -
LWP No. 26) he proposed amending the title to THE RENAISSANCE.   A
SERIES OF STUDIES IN ART AND POETRY, A New Edition, etc.   Hopefully he
added "also, perhaps the price might be raised." (it was, to 10s. 6d.)

Pater niggled and followed the publication with minute attention. "The page might, I think, be shortened by one line. This would increase, instead of slightly diminishing the number of pages in the first edition, besides improving the look of the page, which to my eye is the better for a broad space at the foot" (Jan. 30, 1877: LWP No. 27) On Feb. 24 (LWP No. 29) the proofs were near correction point, but Pater was still bothered about the binding, not liking the ones offered to him. He prepared the advertisement and wanted it inserted in 'your list of forthcoming books' in his 'exact form.' (March 10, 1877: LWP No. 31.

Some details regarding the etching are given in a later letter (March 13, 1877: LWP No. 32): "The Subject of the vignette has no recognised name, being only a small drawing:- the words of the advertisement might rub, - 'with a vignette after Leonardo da Vinci, engraved by Jeens'; and in any gossip on the subject it might be described as being from a favourite drawing by L. da V. in the Louvre". Pater was enchanted by the result and wrote on March 31, 1877 (LWP No. 33 "I have received the proof of the vignette, and think it the most exquisite thing I have seen for a long time - a perfect reproduction of the beauty of the original, and absolutely satisfactory in the exactness and delicacy of its execution. My sincere thanks to Mr. Jeens. I should like to see an impression in red, that I may judge the colour. I suppose it ought to have a morsel of tissue paper inserted to cover it; and lest the monogram should rub it, that must be removed to some other place in the volume." Red it was, and a tissue guard was provided.

When, however, an early printing of the book was sent to him, he replied on April 26th, 1877 (LWP No. 35) with a rush of objections: "I find the binding perfectly satisfactory; with print, paper and vignette it makes a quite typical book. But there are some points to notice - The title-page is insecurely fixed - came out, as you see, without pulling. There is a curious irregularity in the folding of the sheets, which makes the margins unequal, and produces an odd appearance on the upper edge of the volume. Please to notice also the irregularity of pp. VIII and IX; and that the whole of the Preface is printed on a different level from the rest of the book. I trust this is an accident of this particular copy. Alas ! also, for the hands of the book-binders which are apt to tarnish a title-page, and the last page of all, where you will notice also an irregularity similar to that of p. IX. On the title-page, it seems to me that the letters are not bitten in enough. I thought the vignette was to be pasted on, though perhaps it is well enough as it is - looks very beautiful. I think it was a pity the attribution to Leonardo da Vinci was omitted, and that Jeens's o own name might have been much more distinctly visible. Also, in this copy, the vignette is printed awry, and not, ss it ought to be, exactly midway betweenthe printing immediately above and below it.

"Please don't forget my suggestions about advertising and I should be glad if the book could be got out as soon as possible . . . "

A month later the book did come out and it was well and securely bound, but the Preface is slightly out of level with the rest of the book; on the title-page the letters are indeed not bitten in enough; the vignette is not pasted on, the attribution is omitted, the name of the engraver is faint, and it is still printed awry as it is not posed exactly midway between the printing immediately above and below it.

c. Third edition   1888

Title-page:
      THE RENAISSANCE/ STUDIES IN ART AND POETRY/ by/ WALTER PATER/
      Fellow of Brasenose College/ Fourth thousand, revised and enlarged/
      [vignette in red]/ MACMILLAN AND CO./ LONDON AND NEW YORK/ 1888/All
      rights reserved

Imprint:
      p. 252: Printed by R. & R. Clark, Edinburgh

Format:
      Extra crown octavo: 8" x 5¼"

Signatures:
      [A]8   B - Q8   R6

Pagination:
      [i - ix]   x - xvi   [1] 2 - 252

Contents:
      p. [i] half-title: THE RENAISSANCE; [ii] advertisement: By the
      same author,/ MARIUS THE EPICUREAN: His Sensations and Ideas./ 2 /
      vols. Second Edition. 12s/ IMAGINARY PORTRAITS, 6s. / ————— /
      Macmillan and Co. ; [iii] title-page [see above]; [iv] First
      edition printed 1873/ New editions 1877, 1888; [v] dedication/
      ————— / to/ C.L.S./ February, 1873; [vi] blank; [vii] contents;
      [viii] blank; [ix] x - xvi preface; [1] 2 - 252 text with imprint
      [see above] on p. 252

Binding:

Number published and price:
      1,500 at 10s. 6d.

Date of publication:
      January 1888

American edition:
      [1 July 1890]   1000 copies

                  ————————————————

CONTENTS:

      The following alterations from the second edition were made:

      1. "Conclusion" was resored. In a footnote, Pater wrote: "This
brief 'Conclusion' was omitted from the second edition of this book, as
I conceived it might mislead some of those young men into whose hands it
might fall. On the whole, I have thought it best to reprint it here,
with some slight changes which bring it closer to my original meaning.

I have dealt more fully in Marius the Epicurean with the thoughts
suggested by it".

The various versions of the 'Conclusion are compared in Appendix b 2

2. The essay "The School of Giorgione" was added.   This eas first
printed in The Fortnightly Review, 1st October 1877 (See Section I a
No. 24)

On December 1st [1887] Pater wrote the following letter to R. and R
Clark, Edinburgh, printers:

Dear Sirs:
    I send by this post some more copy of the "Renaissance".   I find
your compositor has a way of forcing (I think) every chapter to end at
the end of a page, which seems to me not desirable: and although some
new matter has been added, he has gained by about 4 pages on the original
copy, which, as the book is not a long one, is disadvantageous.   Please
note that the added chapter on The School of Giorgione is to be printed
between those on Leonardo da Vinci and Joachim du Bellay.

Very truly yours

Walter Pater

    It is interesting to note here and elsewhere the care which Pater
took over the details of printing and binding.   With regard to the
above letter:

      1. The third edition has 252 pages, the second only 225

      2. "The School of Giorgione" was placed as Pater requested

      3. The chapters do not all end at the end of a page.

d. Fourth edition   1893

Title-page:
    THE RENAISSANCE/ STUDIES IN ART AND POETRY/ by/ WALTER PATER/ Fellow
    of Brasenose College/ Sixth thousand/ [vignette in red]/ MACMILLAN
    AND CO./ LONDON AND NEW YORK/ 1893/ All rights reserved

Imprint:
    No printer's imprint

Format:
    Extra crown octavo: 8" x 5¼"

Signatures:
    [a] 2   b⁶   B - R⁸

Pagination:
    [i - ix]   x - xvi   [1] 2 - 253   [254-256]

Contents:
    p. [i] half-title: THE RENAISSANCE; [ii] advertisement: By the
    same Author./ MARIUS THE EPICUREAN: His Sensations and Ideas./ ?

vols. Sixth Thosand, Completely Revised. 15s./ IMAGINARY PORTRAITS
A Prince of Court Painters;/ Denys l'Auxerrois; Sebastian van
Storck; Duke Carl/ of Rosenmold. Third Thousand. 6s./
APPRECIATIONS; With an Essay on Style. Third/ Thousand. 8s. 6d.
PLATO AND PLATONISM: A Series of Lectures. 8s. 6d./ MACMILLAN
AND CO.; tissue guard; ⌊iii⌋ title-page ⌊see above⌋; First
Edition printed 1873/ Second 1877, Third 1888, Fourth 1893; ⌊v⌋
dedication/ ——— / to/ C.L.S./ February 1873; [vi] blank; ⌊vii⌋
Contents; ⌊viii⌋ quotation: Yet shall ye be as the wings of a
dove; ⌊ix⌋ x - xvi Preface; ⌊1⌋ 2 - 253 text ; [254-256] blanks

Binding:
    Dark-blue cloth, lettered in gold across spine: The/ RENAISSANCE/
WALTER/ PATER/ MACMILLAN/ AND CO.

Number published and price:
    2,000 at 10s. 6d.

Date of printing:
    26th June 1893 .   Published December 1893

Reprints:
    9th June 1899 - 500 copies

    16th Aug 1900 - 250 copies

American editions:
    16th October 1894   -   1000 copies

    11th March 1897   -   1000 copies

    20th June 1901   -   600 copies

    The following points of difference between the third (1888) and
fourth (1893) editions are noted:

    The advertisement page, title-page sales notice, and editions
statement on verso of the title-page are brought up-to-date in the fourth
edition.

    CONTENTS are the same, but there are slight differences of pagination
These are partly caused by a tendency in the later edition for the text to
be broken up into shorter paragraphs, for example, there are new
paragraphs on p. 4 commencing: "Every one knows the legend of Abelard . .
."and on p. 35: "Far different was the method . . ."

    There are a number of slight differences in the text itself. Thus,
on p. 18 the 3rd edition has: "A new music is arising" while the 4th
edition reads: "A Novel art is arising" In Appendix b 2 a statement
will be found of a collation between the third and fourth edition
printings of the final paper, "Conclusion", which will give an indication
of the extent of the differences of text between these two editions.

    On p. [viii] of the fourth edition we find the quotation: "Yet shall
ye be as the wings of a dove".

    The fourth edition has no printer's imprint.

e. Edition de luxe

    7 June 1900 - 1901
    775 copies at 84/- the set.
    THE RENAISSANCE was volume No. 1

    See No. 15: "Collected editions"

f. Fifth edition

    27th July 1901   500 copies

This edition resembles the 3rd (1888) edition rather than the later 4th (1893) version.

Reprints:

22 July 1902	500	copies
5 May 1904	1000	"
2 Aug. 1906	500	"
19 July 1907	1000	"

American editions:

11 Feb. 1902	500	copies
10 June 1903	500	"
20 June 1904	500	"
5 June 1905	500	"
15 May 1906	500	"
11 Feb. 1907	500	"
5 Mar. 1908	500	"
10 July 1909	500	"

g. New Library Edition

    12 March 1910. Printing ordered.   June 1910: Published.
    1250 copies at 7s. 6d.

    See No. 16 "Collected editions"

h. Thomas Bird Mosher (Portland, Maine, U.S.A.)

    Mosher published THE RENAISSANCE: STUDIES IN ART AND POETRY in two of his series as follows:

Quarto Series. MDCCCCII, xx, 248 p., 11, front (port).
No. IX in the series. $15.00 net
The portrait was taken from a portrait of Pater by Simeon Solomon, dated 1877.
450 copies were printed on hand-made Van Gelder paper

Miscellaneous Series. October MDCCCCXII. xi, 304 p. front.
No. LVII in thr series.
700 copies were printed on Van Gelder paper and 25 numbered copies on Japan vellum.
(second edition published in August 1924).

2.   <u>MARIUS THE EPICUREAN : HIS SENSATIONS AND IDEAS</u>

a. <u>First edition:</u>   1885

<u>Title-page:</u>
    MARIUS THE EPICUREAN/ HIS SENSATIONS AND IDEAS/ by WALTER PATER,
    M.A./ Fellow of Brasenose College, Oxford/ [Greek motto]/ Volume I
    [II]/ LONDON:/ MACMILLAN AND CO./ 1885/ [All rights reserved]

<u>Imprint:</u>
    Volume II p. [247]: Oxford [black letter type]/ Printed by Horace
    Hart, Printer to the University

<u>Format:</u> two volumes; extra crown octavo: 8" x 5¼"

<u>Signatures:</u>
    Vol. I: a_1^4 $B \bar{\underline{2}}B^8$ S^2
        II: a^1 $a \frac{2-4}{}$ $B - Q^8$ R^4

<u>Pagination:</u>
    Vol. I: [i - viii]   [1 - 3]   4 - 260
        II: [i - viii]   [1 - 3]   4 - 246   [247 - 248]

<u>Contents:</u>
    Volume I: p. [i] half-title: MARIUS THE EPICUREAN/ Vol. I; [ii]
    By the same Author./ THE RENAISSANCE: Studies in Art and Poetry./
    2nd Edition, with vignette after Leonardo da Vinci./ 10s. 6d.
    Macmillan and Co.; [iii] title-page (see above); [iv] blank; [v]
    dedication: TO/ HESTER AND CLARA; [vi] blank; [vii] Contents of
    Vol. 1.; [viii] blank; [1] PART THE FIRST; [2] blank; [3]
    4 - 260 text

    Volume II: p. [1] blank; [ii] By the same Author/ THE
    RENAISSANCE: Studies in Art and Poetry./ 2nd Edition, with vignette
    after Leonardo da Vinci./ 10s. 6d. Macmillan and Co.; [iii] Half-
    title: MARIUS THE EPICUREAN; [iv] blank; [v] title-page (see
    above); [vi] blank; [vii] Contents of Vol. II.; [viii] blank; [1]
    PART THE THIRD/ Vol. II; [2] blank; [3] 4 - 246 text; [247] imprint
    (see above); [248] blank

<u>Binding:</u>
    Dark-blue cloth, lettered in gold across spine: MARIUS/ THE/
    EPICUREAN/ VOL. I[II] / WALTER/ PATER/ MACMILLAN/ AND CO.

    Thick ribbed paper

<u>Number published and price:</u>
    1000 at 21s.

<u>Date of publication:</u>
    4th March 1885
    Printed in January; review copies were issued at the end of
    February.

<u>American edition:</u>
    November 1885.   1000 copies

MARIUS was well received by the literary world and prospered from
the date it appeared.   Indeed, Vernon Lee (pseudonym of Miss Violet
Paget) wrote in a postcard to her mother on 21st August, 1891: "None
of my books has sold as much as 1200, America included.   What this
means is shown by Pater's Marius being in the 6th thousand." It seems
that six thousand copies in six years (1885-1891) was a successful
figure.

Pater spent several years in writing Marius. M. Germain d'Hangest
believes that Pater conceived the germ of it in 1878. (Walter Pater:
l'homme et l'oeuvre. Paris 1961, Vol. 1, p. 289.

Vernon Lee spent part of each year in England and wrote assiduously
to her mother, father and step-brother (the poet Eugene Lee-Hamilton)
to report her doings in the English literary world.   Her literary
executor, Miss Irene Cooper Willis published some of these letters in a
privately printed edition in 1937 (Vernon Lee's Letters).   On 20th
July 1881 she wrote: "Pater meditates spending one of his vacations
near Rome, in order to work on his new book on Mythology, so I suppose
we shall see him".   24th July 1882: "By the way I told Pater the idea
(not the plot) [of her book Art and Evolution] and he thought it very
good: and he himself seems to be writing something very similar in the
way of a novel about the time of Marcus Aurelius".

On February 24th, 1883, Pater's sister, Hester, wrote to Vernon Lee:
"Walter enjoyed his visit to Rome very much . . . He was very much
obliged for the introductions you sent him and was very sorry he had no
time to use any. A month is a short time to see much of Rome.   He
found he had to give all his time to the galleries and churches and was
so tired in the evening he was quite unfit for social intercourse".

On July 22nd (1883) in a letter to Vernon Lee, Pater wrote: "I
have hopes of completing one half of my present chief work — an
Imaginary Portrait of a peculiar type of mind in the time of Marcus
Aurelius — by the end of the vacation, and meant to have asked you to
look at some of the MS. perhaps.   I am wishing to get the whole
completed, as I have visions of many smaller pieces of work the
composition of which would be actually pleasanter to me.   However I
regard this present matter as a sort of duty.   For, you know, I think
that there is a fourth sort of religious phase possible for the modern
mind, over and above those presented in your admirable paper in the
Contemporary, the conditions of which phase it is the main object of my
design to convey".   (LWP No. 78)

In a letter dated 20th June 1884, Miss Paget wrote: "The Paters are
most kind.   Each afternoon I have had a long audience in his study on
account of his lamness (gout) & he had read me part of his philosophica
romance about the time of the Antonines.   Fine, but I think lacking in
vitality".

Finally, on 4 Dec. (1884) Pater wrote to Miss Paget: "I am very
busy correcting the proofs of my new book". (LWP No. 83)

William Sharp in his Papers Critical and Reminiscent (Heinemann
1912) wrote, pp. 211-212: "My chief treasure is the bound copy of the
proofs of Marius the Epicurean. I had these proofs for some weeks
before publication, and so had the additional pleasure of a thorough
familiarity with one of the finest, and perhaps the most distinctive of

MARIUS THE EPICUREAN

HIS SENSATIONS AND IDEAS

BY

WALTER PATER, M.A.

FELLOW OF BRASENOSE COLLEGE, OXFORD.

Χειμερινὸς ὄνειρος, ὅτε μήκισται αἱ νύκτες.

VOLUME I.

SECOND EDITION.

LONDON:

MACMILLAN AND CO.

1885.

of the prose works of the Victorian era, before the less fortunate
public knew anything of it.   <u>Marius</u> had been begun, and in part written
long before Walter Pater went to Rome, in 1882, for the first time;   but
it was not till the summer of 1883 that he wrote it as it now stands —
wrote and rewrote, with infinite loving care for every idea, for every
phrase, for each sentence, each epithet, each little word or mark of
punctuation".

The New Library edition (1910) gave the dates 1881-1884.

It is interesting to note that Pater proposed that <u>Marius</u> should
appear serially in <u>Macmillan's Magazine</u>.   There is a letter dated Sept.
9, 1884 to Alexander Macmillan in which he says: "I was not surprised
that Morley (editor) was unable to take my MS for the magazine, its
unfitness for serial publication having sometimes occurred to me . . .
I am now thinking of offering it to a publisher with a view to its
appearing in the spring.   I should feel much honoured if you would take
it.   It would be pleasing to me in many ways; and the convenience of
printing in Oxford, great". (<u>LWP</u> No. 81).

b. <u>Second edition:</u>   1885

<u>Title-page:</u>
MARIUS THE EPICUREAN/ HIS SENSATIONS AND IDEAS/ by/ WALTER PATER, M.
A./ Fellow of Brasenose College, Oxford./ [Greek motto]/ Volume I.
[II.]/ <u>Second edition</u>./ LONDON:/ MACMILLAN AND CO./ 1885/ [All rights
reserved]

<u>Imprints:</u>
I. pp. [4] and 239: <u>Printed by</u> R. & R. Clark, <u>Edinburgh.</u>

II. pp. [4] and 218:   – do. –

<u>Format:</u>
two volumes; extra crown octavo: 8" x 5"

<u>Signatures:</u>
I. [B] C – Q^8
II. [B] C – O^8 P^4 Q^2

<u>Pagination:</u>
I. [1 – 11]   12 – 239 [240]
II. [1 – 9]   10 – 218 [219 – 220]

<u>Contents:</u>
<u>Volume I:</u>
p. [1] half-title: MARIUS THE EPICUREAN; [2] advertisement: <u>By</u>
<u>the same Author</u>./ THE RENAISSANCE: Studies in Art and Poetry/ <u>Second</u>
<u>Edition, with vignette after Leonardo da Vinci</u>./ 10s. 6d./. Macmillan
and Co. ; title-page (see above); [4] publisher's device: intertwined M. M. & Co./ <u>third thousand</u>/ imprint (see above); [5]
dedication: TO/ HESTER AND CLARA; [6] blank; [7] CONTENTS. ;
[8] blank; [9] PART THE FIRST. ; [10] blank; [11] 12 – 239

text and imprint (see above); [240] blank

Volume II:
p. [1] half-title: MARIUS THE EPICUREAN. ; [2] publisher's
device: intertwined M. M. & Co. ; [3] title-page (see above);
[4]: third thousand./ imprint (see above); [5] CONTENTS; [6]
blank; [7] PART THE THIRD. ; [8] blank; [9] 10 - 218 text and
imprint (see above); [219 - 220 blanks

Binding:
Olive-green half linen, with cream spines; paper labels: MARIUS/
THE/ EPICUREAN/ Vol. I [II] / WALTER/ PATER *

Paper with edges untrimmed at sides and lower edges

Number published and price:
2000 at 12s. 0d.

Date published
12 November 1885

American edition:
8 December 1890. 1000 copies

---

* This is unique in binding style among Pater's works published in his
lifetime.   Macmillan proposed for the second edition a less expensive
edition, in one or two volumes.   Pater suggested (16 June 1885: LWP No.
91) two volumes and tried, with success, to have something quite
different in style from the first edition.   In the same letter he was
"pleased to hear that the first edition of Marius is allbut exhausted".
He requested that this edition should be printed by "Clark, or your
London printers ?   I think the Oxford printing, as exemplified in the
first edition, far from what it might be."   In deference to Pater's
wishes the printing of the first edition was entrusted to R. & R. Clark
of Edinburgh.

Pater thought that the second edition of Marius "a very pretty-
looking pair of volumes." (LWP No. 96)

On August 9th (1885) Pater wrote to a great friend, M.E. Grant Duff
(later Sir Mountstuart Grant Duff) as follows:

"Accept one line of sincere thanks for your kind appreciation
"of my work - appreciation which I greatly value.   There were
"some tiresome misprints, and some mistakes, in the first
"edition of 'Marius', which I have corrected in the second
"edition, which I hope will soon be ready".   (LWP No. 92)

A comparison of the second edition with the first shows that no
searching revision was undertaken; some slight variations of wording
and punctuation were made.   The most significant alteration was that
the passage commencing in the first edition, Vol. II, p. 96: "It was
then that the good man's son . . . " and finishing on the same page:
within the red-hot iron door" was omitted, doubtless by reason of
its distressing nature.

The second edition has the same chapter headings as the first, with
two slight alterations:

1. Volume I Chapter XIII: the quotation marks around
   "Mistress and Mother" are not in the first edition;

2. Volume II Chapter XVIII: the quotation marks around
   "The Ceremony of the Dart" are not in the first edition.

c. <u>Third edition</u>   1892

<u>Title-page</u>:
    MARIUS THE EPICUREAN/ HIS SENSATIONS AND IDEAS/ by/ WALTER PATER/
    Fellow of Brasenose College/ [motto in Greek] / Volume I [II]/
    Sixth thousand completely revised/ London/ MACMILLAN AND CO./ and
    New York/ 1892/ [All rights reserved]

<u>Imprints</u>:
    I. p. [iv]: Oxford: Horace Hart, Printer to the University

    II. p. [vi]: Oxford [in black letter type] Horace Hart, Printer to the
                 University

<u>Format</u>:
    Extra crown octavo: 8" x 5 3/8"
    Two volumes

<u>Signatures</u>:
    [A]4 B - R^8 S^6 Volume I
    [A]4 B - Q^8 R^4 II

<u>Pagination</u>:
    [i - viii]   [1 - 3]   4 - 265   [266 - 268] Volume I
    [i - viii]   [1 - 3]   4 - 246   [247 - 248]   II

<u>Contents</u>:
        Volume I:
    p. [i] half title: <u>MARIUS THE EPICUREAN</u>; [ii] advertisements: <u>By</u>
    <u>the same Author</u>./ THE RENAISSANCE: Studies in Art and Poetry, Fourth/
    thousand, Revised and Enlarged. 10s. 6d./ IMAGINARY PORTRAITS: A
    Prince of Court Painters;/ Denys l'Auxerrois; Sebastian van Storck;
    Duke Carl/of Rosenmold. Third thousand 6s./ APPRECIATIONS: with an
    Essay on Style. Third thousand. 8s. 6d./ MACMILLAN AND CO. ; [iii]
    title-page (see above); [iv]: <u>First Edition Printed February</u> 1885/
    <u>Second</u>, November 1885, <u>Third</u> 1892/ [short rule] / imprint (see above)
    [v] dedication: TO/ HESTER AND CLARA; [vi] blank; [vii] Contents
    of Volume I; [viii] blank; [1] <u>PART THE FIRST</u>/ Vol. I; [2] blank
    [3] 4 - 265 text; [266 - 268] blanks

        Volume II
    pp. [i - ii] blanks; [iii] half title: <u>MARIUS THE EPICUREAN</u>; [iv]
    advertisement: <u>By the same Author</u>. [as in Vol. I]; [v] title-
    page)see above); [vi] imprint (see above); [vii] Contents of Vol.
    II; [viii] blank; [1] <u>PART THE THIRD</u>; [2] blank; [3] 4 -
    246 text; [247 - 248] blanks

<u>Binding</u>:
    Smooth dark blue cloth; lettered in gold across spines: MARIUS/THE/

EPICUREAN/ Vol. I [II] / WALTER/ PATER/ MACMILLAN/ AND CO.

Number published and price:
   2,000 copies at 15s. 0d.

Date of publication:
   10th August 1892
   Printed June 1892

   Reprint:
   31 January 1896   500 copies

   American editions:
   12 January 189 3   1,000 copies
   24 May 1895   5oo   "
   11 March 1897   1,000   "

More than 6,000 textual changes were made in the third edition. For a detailed and interesting survey of the changes made by Pater reference should be made to : Edmund Chandler. Pater on Style: An examination of the essay on 'Style' and the textual history of 'Marius the Epicurean' [Anglistica] Vol. XI. Rosenhilde & Bagger, Copenhagen. 1958. This work originated as a thesis accepted by the University of London for a M.A. degree 1954. Birbeck College. Chandler states that the later edition of Marius amounted to a "total rewriting" and suggests that this was done to illustrate the views on writing which Pater pronounced in the essay on "Style" (APPRECIATIONS WITH AN ESSAY ON STYLE 1889)

The third edition shows twelve changes in chapter headings:

Chapter	Second edition	Third edition
III	Dilexi Decorem Domus Tuae	Change of Air
IV	O Mare, O Litus, Verum Secretumque Moyzeion	The Tree of Knowledge
VII	Pagan Death	A Pagan End
VIII	Animula, Vagula, Blandula !	Animula Vagula
X	Mirum est ut Animus Agitatione Motuque Corporis excitetur	On the way
XI	The most religious City in the world	"The most religious City in the world"
XII	The Divinity that doth hedge a King	"The Divinity that doth hedge a King"
XVII	Many Prophets and Kings have desired to see the things which ye see	Beata Urbs
XIX	Paratum Cor meum, Deus !	The Will as Vision
XXII	The minor "Peace of the Church"	"The minor Peace of the Church"
XXIII	Sapientia aedicavit sibi Domum	Divine Service

Chapter	Second edition	Third edition
XXVI	Ah! Voilà les Âmes qu'il falloit à la mienne !	The Martyrs

d. **Fourth edition:**   1898

Title-page:
MARIUS/ THE EPICUREAN/ HIS SENSATIONS AND IDEAS/ by/ WALTER PATER/
Fellow of Brasenose College/ [motto in Greek]/ Volume I [II]/
MACMILLAN AND CO., Limited/ St. Martin's Street, London/ 1898

Imprints:
Volume I. p. [243]: Printed by R. & R. Clark, Limited, Edinburgh

II. p. [224]   - do. -

Signatures:
I. [A]^4 B - Q^8 R^2

II. [A]^4 B - P^8

Pagination:
I. [i - viii]   [1 - 2]   3 - 242   [243 - 244]

II. [i - viii]   [1 - 2]   3 - 223   [224]

Contents:
Volume I:

p. [i] half-title: MARIUS THE EPICUREAN; [ii] advertisement: By
Walter Pater; [iii] title-page (see above); [iv] First Edition,
February 1885./ Second Edition, November 1885./ Third Edition, 1892.
/Fourth Edition, 1898; [v] dedication: TO/ HESTER AND CLARA;
[vi] blank; [vii] CONTENTS/ PART THE FIRST . . . PART THE SECOND .
. . ; [viii] blank; [1] PART THE FIRST; [2] blank; 3 - 242
[243] text with imprint (see above0 on p. [243]; [244] blank

Volume II:

pp. [i - ii] blanks; [iii] half-title: MARIUS THE EPICUREAN; [iv]
advertisement: By Walter Pater; [v] title-page (see above);
[vi] First Edition, February 1885/ Second Edition, November 1885/
Third Edition 1892/ Fourth Edition, 1898; [vii] CONTENTS/PART THE
THIRD . . . PART THE FOURTH . . . ; [viii] blank; [1] PART THE
THIRD; [2] blank; 3 - 223 [224] text with imprint (see above? on
p. [224]

Binding:
Dark blue cloth; lettered in gold across spine: MARIUS/ THE/
EPICUREAN/ Vol. I [II]/ WALTER/ PATER/ MACMILLAN/ AND CO.

Thick ribbed paper

Number published:
500 copies

Date of publication:

1898 (printing ordered 19 November 1897)

Reprints:

8 March 1899	250 copies	5 February 1901	250 copies
23 February 1900	250 copies		
3 January 1901	350 copies		

American editions:

27 March 1899	250 copies
9 June 1899	500 copies
20 June 1901	500 copies

The fourth edition shows two changes in chapter headings:

Chapter	Third Edition	Fourth Edition
XX	Guests	20. Two Curious Houses - 1. Guests
XX1	The Church in Cecilia's House	21. Two Curious Houses - 2. The Church Cecilia's House

The chapter numbers in the fourth and succeeding editions have been changed from Roman to Arabic numerals (1 - 28)

---

e. Edition de Luxe

7 June 1900

775 copies at 84/- the set

MARIUS THE EPICUREAN NUMBERED Volumes II and III of the set

See No. 15: "Collected editions"

---

f. Thomas Bird Mosher (Boston, Mass. U.S.A.) published this work in full in two octavo volumes in 1900. Vol. I carried a foreword by William Marion Rudy, and Vol. II a note by Richard le Gallienne; 450 copies on Van Gelder hand-made paper, 35 numbered copies on Japan vellum and 4 copies on pure Roman vellum in folded sheets unbound. This was a publication in the Mosher Quarto series, VIII. $15.00 ea.

Mosher, most indefatigable of pirates, published extracts from MARIUS:

(1) "A Discourse of Marcus Aurelius" with an introduction by himself in the Bibelot, I (April 1895), 77 - ⌊106⌋. This is chapter XII: The Divinity that doth hedge a king.

(2) "Story of Cupid and Psyche done out of the Latin of Apuleius by Walter Pater" (April 1897), 53 pages. "This edition of Cupid and Psyche is a faithful reprint of the original text found in Marius the Epicurean (London 1855), 425 copies of this book have been printed on Japan vellum at the press of George B. Loring, Portland, Maine (Brocade series, IV" At least 6 editions of this slender volume were published

78

by Mosher, the sixth being issued in January 1909.

(3) "Two Chapters from Marius the Epicurean". These were Chapter VI "Euphism" and Chapter 7 "Pagan Death". This, again, is from the Bibelot, XVIII, October 1912, pp. 349 - [384]

---

g. Fifth edition: 1902

   6 November 1901 (published February 1902)   500 copies

   Reprints:

21 August 1902	500 copies
9 January 1903	500 copies
20 July 1904	1,000 copies
11 October 1906	1,000 copies
6 April 1909	1,000 copies

   American editions:

21 August 1902	500 copies
24 June 1903	500 copies
1 March 1905	500 copies
24 April 1908	500 copies

---

h. Faith and Freedom Pamphlets

   "The Church of Cecilia's House" by Walter Pater
   (Reprinted by kind permission of Messrs Macmillan from Pater's "Marius the Epicurean")

   London: S.C. Brown Langham & Company Ltd. 1903. Price threepence.

   (This comprises the whole of Chapter XXI of MARIUS THE EPICUREAN)

---

i. New Library Edition

   12 March 1910   Printing ordered.   June 1910: Published

   1250 copies at 7s. 6d.

   See No. 16: "Collected Editions"

j. Special editions:

   The following editions, though outside the scope of this bibliography, are noted for their special interest:

   (1) A 2 volume Limited Edition, t.e.g. holland backs, was published by the Medici Society in 1913

   (2) Messrs Macmillan published an edition in New York, 1926, 12mo. xix 348 pp. This edition was edited by Anne Kimball Tuell, and contained numerous notes, particularly on the sources of the work.

(3) In 1908, Macmillan and Co. published a superb limited edition
(325 copies), 2 vols. xxvii + 144 pp. and viii + 123 pp.,
Royal Quarto, 12" x 9", priced £12. 12. 0d.   J.C. Squire
contributed an introductory essay: "Pater and Marius", and the
volumes were illustrated with sixteen admirable plates in dry
point by Thomas Mackenzie. This edition was printed in Great
Britain on English hand-made paper, t.e.g., others uncut, The
University Press, Oxford. The binding is of white vellum with
batik paper sides and the paper is of exceptional quality.

In a letter from Brasenose College, dated January 28th (1886) to
Carl W. Ernest (American writer), Pater states: "I may add that 'Marius
is designed to be the first of a kind of trilogy, or triplet, of works
of a similar character; dealing with the same problems, under altered
historical conditions. The period of the second of the series would be
at the end of the 16th century, and the place France: of the third, the
time, probably the end of the last century - and the scene, England."

There is an intersting note in <u>Notes and Queries</u> July 17, 1893, under
the heading "Walter Pater's Autograph". "In answer to a request that he
should write a favourite sentiment from his own writings for a collection
of autographs, Mr. Pater wrote the following: "And we too desire not a
fair one, but the fairest of all. Unless we find him, we shall think we
have failed." The words were from Lucian. See <u>Marius</u> p. 179, first
edition. The date 28th Oct. 1888. Charles Hiatt."

It may be of interest to note that the following books were in
Pater's library:

Lettres de Marc Aurele et de Fronton, 2 vols. (1830)

Le Livre de Marc Aurele (Lyon: 1544).

Both books bear Pater's signature.

a. First edition

Title-page:
    IMAGINARY PORTRAITS/ by/ WALTER PATER, M.A./ Fellow of Brasenose
    College, Oxford/ London/ MACMILLAN AND CO./ and New York/ 1887/
    All rights reserved

Imprints:
    p. [iv] and p. 180: Printed by R. & R. Clark, Edinburgh

Format:
    Extra crown octavo   8" x 5$\frac{1}{4}$"

Signatures:
    [A] 4   B - M^8 N^4
Pagination:
    [viii]   [1] 2 - 180   [181 - 184]

Contents:
    p. [i] half title: IMAGINARY PORTRAITS; [ii] advertisement: By
    the same Author./ THE RENAISSANCE: Studies in Art and Poetry. Second
    /Edition, with Vignette, after Leonardo da Vinci. 10s. 6d./ MARIUS
    THE EPICUREAN: His Sensations and Ideas./ 2 vols. Second Edition.
    12s./ [short rule] / MACMILLAN AND CO. ; [iii] title-page (see above
    [iv] imprint (see above); [v] CONTENTS; [vi] blank; [vii]
    divisional title: I/ A PRINCE OF COURT PAINTERS; [viii] blank;
    [1] 2 - 180 text with imprint (see above) on p. 180; [181 - 184]
    advertisements: MESSRS. MACMILLAN AND CO.'S PUBLICATIONS.

    Other divisional titles: p. [49] DENYS L'AUXERROIS; [89] III/
    SEBASTIAN VAN STORCK; [135] IV/ DUKE CARL OF ROSENMOLD

Binding:
    Dark blue cloth. Lettered in gold across spine: IMAGINARY/
    PORTRAITS/ WALTER/ PATER/ MACMILLAN/ AND CO.

    Paper of varying widths

Number published and price:
    1,000 at 6s.

Date of publication:
    24th May 1887 *

CONTENTS:

    All four items in this book had previously appeared in Macmillan's
Magazine. They are listed below in the order of the book, with periodic-
al dates.   The numbers given are those of the CHRONOLOGICAL RECORD,
Section Ia.

---

* The date of actual publication is confirmed in a letter Pater
wrote to William Sharp on 23rd May (1887) in which he said: "My book
will be out tomorrow, and I have directed a copy of it to be sent to
you, which please accept with very kind regards. I pondered the
inclusion among the other pieces of the 'Child in the House', but
found it would need many alterations, which I felt disinclined to make
just then. I hope it may be included in some future similar series."
(LWP No. 107)

Much earlier Pater had written to another friend, John Miller Gray
saying: "I am very pleased to hear of your continued memory and
interest in my projected series of Imaginary Portraits, one of which I
have now seriously on hand. I have been looking over it, but find it
is still too much a matter of shorthand notes at present, or I would
very gladly send it to you, and should value your remarks upon it . ."
(November, 1881 ?)   (LWP No. 64)

We cannot be certain here whether Pater was referring to a major
work such as MARIUS or to a projected series of minor portraits. It
seems too earlier for the larger work, which would surely not be in
draft state at the time, and he may be referring to "An English Poet"
(see No. 29).

A very useful summary of Pater's various Imaginary Portraits, both
projected and completed, will be found in the Introduction to
Imaginary Portraits by Walter Pater, Eugene J. Brzenk (Harper and Row.
New York: 1964).

b. Second Edition   1890

Title-page:
        IMAGINARY PORTRAITS/ by WALTER PATER/ Fellow of Brasenose College/
        Third thousand/ LONDON [Black letter type]/ MACMILLAN AND CO./ and
        New York/ 1890/ All rights reserved

Imprint:
        p. 180: Printed by R. & R. Clark, Edinburgh

Format:
        Extra crown octavo   8" x 5¼"

Signatures:
        [A] 4   B – M^8 N^2

Pagination:
        [i – viii]   [1] 2 – 180

Contents:
        p. [i] half-title: IMAGINARY PORTRAITS; [ii] advertisement:
        By the same Author./ THE RENAISSANCE: Studies in Art and Poetry.

Fourth/ Thousand: Revised and Enlarged. 10s. 6d./ MARIUS THE
EPICUREAN: His Sensations and Ideas,/ 2 vols. Second Edition.
12s./ APPRECIATIONS: with an Essay on Style. Third Thousand./
8s. 6d./ [short rule] / MACMILLAN AND CO.; [iii] title-page (see
above); [iv] blank; [v] CONTENTS; [vi] blank; [vii]
Divisional fly title: I/ A PRINCE OF COURT PAINTERS; [viii]
blank; [1] 2 - 180 text with imprint (see above) at foot of p.
180

64 pp. "Catalogue of Books/ published by/ MACMILLAN AND CO./
Bedford Street, Covent Garden, London/ . . . appended.

Other divisional fly titles: p. [49] DENYS L'AUXERROIS; [89]
III/ SEBASTIAN VAN STORCK; [135] IV/ DUKE CARL OF ROSENMOLD

Binding:
Dark blue cloth.
Lettered in gold across spine: IMAGINARY/ PORTRAITS/ WALTER/ PATER
/ MACMILLAN AND CO.

Paper of varying widths

Number published and price:
1250 copies at 6s.

Date of Publication:
March 1891
Printing ordered November 1890

Reprint:
19th October 1894. 1000 copies

Though Pater revised the text for this edition, the differences
between the first and second editions are only slight in nature and
not significant. A few illustrative examples are given from the
the first portrait:

Page	First edition	Second edition
11	Rubens	Peter Paul Rubens
17	This letter discloses	This letter really discloses
21	new style	"new style"
29	His animals	The animals in his pictures
39	Paris	Paris* [f.n.] Possibly written at this date, but almost certainly not printed till many years later — Note in Second Edition.

There are slight differences in setting out the type which are not
sufficient to alter the pagination.

---

c. Third edition :

1 May 1896   500 copies

Some slight re-arrangement of type but no significant differences between this and the second edition. Printing revises concern advertisements, notifications of editions published, and publisher's monogram printed in this edition on verso of half-title.

Reprint:

8 March 1899   250 copies

American edition:

10 January 1899   500 copies

d. Edition de Luxe:

7 June 1900
775 copies at 84/- the set

Vol. Iv comprised IMAGINARY PORTRAITS and GASTON DE LATOUR

See No. 15 "Collected editions"

e. Fourth edition:

1 January 1901   [500] copies

Reprints:

9 June 1903   500 copies
11 September 1905   500 copies
8 January 1907   500 copies
13 November 1909 500 copies

American editions:

31 October 1902   500 copies
 5 June 1905   500 copies
 9 October 1907   500 copies

f. New Library Edition:

12 March 1910   Printing ordered.   July 1910: Published

1250 copies at 7s. 6d.

See No. 16: "Collected Editions"

g. Foreign translation:

Portraits Imaginaires traduction de Georges Khnopff. Introduction d' Arthur Symons (Paris: Mercure de France: Jan. 1900). 1 vol. in 12. 248 pp.

4.   APPRECIATIONS: WITH AN ESSAY ON STYLE

a. First edition   1889

Title-page:
    APPRECIATIONS/ WITH AN ESSAY ON STYLE/ by/ WALTER PATER/ Fellow of
    Brasenose College/ LONDON [black letter type]/ MACMILLAN AND CO./
    and New York/ 1889 / All rights reserved

Imprint:
    At foot of p. 264: Printed by R. & R. Clark, Edinburgh.

Format:
    Extra crown octavo   8" x 5 3/8"

Signatures:
    [A] 4   B - R⁸   S⁴

Pagination:
    [viii]   [1] 2 - 264

Contents:
    p. [i] half-title: APPRECIATIONS; [ii] advertisement: By the
    same Author./ THE RENAISSANCE: Studies in Art and Poetry. Fourth
    /Thousand, Revised and enlarged. 10s. 6d./ MARIUS THE EPICUREAN:
    His Sensations and Ideas./ 2 vols. Second Edition. 12s. /
    IMAGINARY PORTRAITS: A Prince of Court Painters;/ Denys l'Auxerro
    is; Sebastian van Storck; Duke Carl/of Rosenmold. 6s./ [short
    rule]/ MACMILLAN AND CO;[iii]title-page(see above); [iv] blank;
    [v] dedication: To the Memory of my Brother/ William Thompson
    Pater/ who quitted a useful and happy life/ Sunday April 24 1887/
    Requiem eternam Dona ei Domine/ et Lux perpetua luceat ei; [vi]
    blank; [vii] CONTENTS; [viii] blank; [1] 2 - 264 text with
    imprint (see above0 at foot of p. 264

Binding:
    Dark blue cloth.   Lettered in gold across spine: APPRECIATIONS/
    WITH AN ESSAY/ ON STYLE/ WALTER/ PATER/ MACMILLAN/ AND CO.

Number published and price:
    1,000 at 8s. 6d.

Date of publication:
    15th November 1889

    Pater wrote to the printers Messrs. R. & R. Clark (c. 20 June
1889: LWP No. 156) as follows: "Messrs Macmillan propose that you
should print a book of mine, for publication by Nov. 1st, to be
entitled,
                    'On Style,
                With other studies in literature'.
The volume to be precisely similar, in all respects, to the edition of
'The Renaissance', printed by you, in 1888. I am anxious to finish
the correction of proofs, and get the whole ready, for Press by
August 8th; after which I propose to leave England for some weeks.
I send, by this post, the first portion of the copy, and will send the
remainder in good time . . ."

CONTENTS:

This book contains a collection of papers most of which had previously been published in periodicals. Titles and periodical references are given below, together with the number in the CHRONOLOGICAL RECORD, Section Ia

as "A Fragment on <u>Measure for Measure</u>

No acknowledgements were made or any statement that the contents
had been printed earlier. The dates of the original printings were
however given at the end of each article.

"STYLE" : Periodical and book versions

In general the differences are not many and are of little
significance. There are small alterations which tend to expand the
expression in the book version (Pater's revisions nearly always were more
diffuse than the originals). A few instances are given below:

<u>Fortnightly Review</u>	APPRECIATIONS
"in the severance of an obscure complex into its parts or phrases"	"in the resolution of an obscure and complex object into its component parts"
"who can tell how and where"	"who can tell where and to what extent"
"more beautiful to him"	"more beautiful to the writer himself"

Certain references to an article by George Saintsbury which
appeared in the periodical were omitted in <u>APPRECIATIONS</u>.

"POSTCRIPT" and "ROMANTICISM"

A number of revisions were made in the later "Postcript" version.
They were mostly slight: various alterations in punctuation which, by

inserting parenthetical dashes and commas, tended to make the reading
easier; different illustrative writers were named (e.g. Victor Hugo
for Charles Baudelaire); topical mentions of work by John Morley
omitted; and in APPRECIATIONS a final paragraph - "Material for the
artist . . . the vulgarity which is dead to form" was added. The
last difference is the only one of any significance.

---

b. Second edition   1890

Title-page:
    APPRECIATIONS/ WITH AN ESSAY ON STYLE/ by WALTER PATER/ Fellow of
    Brasenose College/ Third Thousand/ LONDON (black letter type/
    MACMILLAN AND CO./ and New York/ 1890/ All rights reserved

Imprint:
    At foot of p. 274: Printed by R. & R. Clark, Edinburgh

Format:
    Extra crown octavo   8" x 5 3/8"

Signatures:
    [A]^6 B - S^8 [T]^2

Pagination:
    [i - viii]   [1] 2 - 274   [275 - 280]

Contents:
    p. ⌊ i ⌋ half-title: APPRECIATIONS; ⌊ii⌋ advertisement: By the
    same Author./ THE RENAISSANCE; Studies in Art and Poetry. Fourth/
    Thousand, Revised and Enlarged.   10s. 6d./ MARIUS THE EPICUREAN:
    His Sensations and Ideas./ 2 vols. Second Edition. 12s./ IMAGINARY
    PORTRAITS: A Prince of Court Painters; Denys l'Auxerrois;
    Sebastian van Storck; Duke Carl/ of Rosenmold. 6s./ [Short rule]/
    MACMILLAN AND CO.; ⌊iii⌋ title-page (see above); ⌊iv⌋ First
    Edition 1889/ Second Edition 1890; ⌊ v ⌋ dedication: To the
    Memory of my.Brother/ William Thompson Pater/ who quitted a
    useful and happy life/ Sunday April 24 1887/ Requiem eternam Dona
    ei Domine/ et Lux perpetua luceat Ei/ ⌊vi⌋ blank; ⌊vii⌋ CONTENTS
    [viii] blank; [1] 2 - 274 text with imprint (see above) at foot
    of p. 274; ⌊275 - 280⌋ advertisements: Messrs Macmillan's
    publications

Binding:
    Dark blue cloth
    Lettered in gold across spine: APPRECIATIONS/ WALTER/ PATER/
    MACMILLAN/ AND CO.

    In the second and subsequent editions, "With an Essay on Style"
    was omitted from the lettering on the spine

Number published and price:
    1,500 copies at 8s. 6d.

<u>Date of publication</u>:
 May 1890

<u>Reprint</u>:
 25 November 1894   1,000 copies

<u>American edition</u>:
 1 July 189o   1,000 cppies

<u>CONTENTS</u>:

 These were the same, and in the same order, as with the First
edition (1889) with the following exceptions:

 1. "Aesthetic Poetry" was omitted
    Michael Field (in the person of Miss Katherine Bradley) wrote
    in her journal on 25th August 1890: "He ⌊Pater⌋ has struck out
    the <u>Essay on Aesthetic Poetry</u> in <u>Appreciations</u> because it gave
    offence to some pious person – he is getting hopelessly prudish
    in literature and defers to the moral weaknesses of everybody.
    Deplorable ! " (Michael Field. <u>Works and Days</u> (Murray 1933),119

 2. "Feulillet's 'La Morte' " was inserted between "Dante Gabriel
    Rossetti" and "Postcript".   This unsigned review first
    appeared in <u>Macmillan's Magazine</u> (Dec. 1886) See Section I a
    No. 45

 3. "Shakespere's English Kings" in the first edition became
    "Shakespeare's English Kings" in the second.

---

c. <u>Third edition</u>

  3 January 1895 (printed)   500 copies

  <u>Reprints</u>:

     14 January   1897   250 copies
      1 July   1897   500   "
     20 December 1897   500   "
     21 March   1900   500   "

  <u>American edition</u>:

     25 October   1898   500 copies
     20 June   1901   500   "

d. <u>Edition de Luxe</u>
                  1901
     775 copies at 84/- the set
     <u>APPRECIATIONS</u> was no. V of the set.

     See No. 15 "Collected editions"

3. <u>Fourth edition</u>

  7 October 1901   500 copies

  <u>Reprints</u>:

```
        9 October 1903        1,000 copies
       12 June 1907           1,000    "
```

Americon editions:

```
        5 May         1902      500 copies
       25 September   1903      500    "
       29 December    1904      500    "
       10 February    1906      500    "
       26 February    1907      500    "
       16 April       1908      500    "
       30 November    1909      500    "
```

f. New Library Edition:

```
       30 June        1910    Printing ordered.  August 1910: Published
```
1250 copies at 7s. 6d.

See No. 16 "Collected Editions"

a. First edition   1893

Title-page:
    PLATO AND PLATONISM/ A SERIES OF LECTURES/ by/ WALTER PATER/Fellow
    of Brasenose College/ [motto in Greek]/ London/ MACMILLAN AND CO./
    and New York/ 1893/ [All rights reserved]

Imprints:
    p. [iv]: Oxford: _Horace Hart, Printer to the University
    p. [260]: Oxford [black letter type]/ Horace Hart, Printer to the
              University

Format:
    Extra crown octavo   8" x 5 3/8"

Signatures:
    [A] 4   B - R^8 S^2

Pagination:
    [viii]   [1] 2 - 259   [260]

Contents:
    p. [i] half-title: PLATO AND PLATONISM; [ii] advertisement: By
    the same Author./ THE RENAISSANCE: Studies in Art and Poetry.
    Fourth/ Thousand, Revised and enlarged. 10s. 6d./ APPRECIATIONS:
    With an Essay on Style.   Third Thousand./ 8s. 6d./ MARIUS THE
    EPICUREAN: His Sensations and Ideas./ 2 vols.   Sixth Thousand,
    Completely Revised.   15s. / IMAGINARY PORTRAITS: A Prince of
    Court Painters; / Denys l'Auxerrois; Sebastian van Storck; Duke
    Carl of/ Rosenmold.   Third Thousand.   6s./ MACMILLAN AND CO. ;iii
    title-page (see above)iv Publisher's device formed of intertwined
    M. M. & Co. / Printer's imprint at foot (see above); [v] Note
    by the Author: "The Lectures of which this volume is composed . .
    . his own writings"/ W.P. [taking 8 lines plus author's initials];
    [vi] blank; [vii] CONTENTS; [viii] blank; [1] 2 - 259 text; [260]
    printer's imprint (see above)

Binding:
    Dark blue cloth
    Lettered in gold across spine: PLATO/ AND PLATONISM/ WALTER/ PATER
    / MACMILLAN/ AND CO.

Number published and price:
    2,000 at 8s. 6d.

Date of Publication:
    9th February 1893
    Printing ordered December 1892

CONTENTS

    The book was based on a series of lectures given at Oxford 1891 -92
See Appendix c. 1. for a note on Pater as a lecturer.

    Three of the chapters had been printed earilerin periodicals; the
others were here printed for the first time.

The periodical, title and date issued are given, where applicable,
together with the number in the CHRONOLOGICAL RECORD, Section I a

Lecture		Section I a
I.	Plato and the Doctrine of Motion Macmillan's Magazine (May 1892) as "A Chapter on Plato"	No. 81
II.	Plato and the Doctrine of Rest	
III.	Plato and the Doctrine of Number	
IV.	Plato and Socrates	
V.	Plato and the Sophists	
VI.	The Genius of Plato The Contemporary Review (Feb. 1892)	80
VII.	The Doctrine of Plato 1. The Thoery of Ideas 2. Dialectic	
VIII.	Lacedaemon The Contemporary Review (June 1892)	82
IX.	The Republic	
X.	Plato's Aesthetics	

b. Second edition   1895

Title-page:

PLATO AND PLATONISM/ A SERIES OF LECTURES/ by/ WALTER PATER/ Fellow
of Brasenose College/ [motto in Greek]/ LONDON (black letter type)/
MACMILLAN AND CO. Limited/ New York: The Macmillan Company/ 1895/
All rights reserved

Imprint:
None

Format:
Extra crown octavo   8" x 5 3/8"

Signatures:
[A]⁴   B - R⁸

Pagination:
[i - vi]   vii   [viii]   1 - 256

Contents:
p. [i] half-title: PLATO AND PLATONISM; [ii] advertisement:
By the same Author; [iii] title-page (see above); [iv] First

Edition 1893. Second Edition 1895; [v] Note by the Author: "The
Lectures of which this volume is composed . . . his own writings./
W.P. " [taking 8 lines plus author's initials]; [vi] blank;
vii CONTENTS; [viii] blank; 1 - 256 text

Binding:
    Dark blue cloth
    Lettered in gold across spine: PLATO/ AND PLATONISM/ WALTER/ PATER
    / MACMILLAN/ AND CO.

Number published and price:
    250 c copies at 8s. 6d.

Date of Printing:

    17 May 1895

Reprints:

    26 August   1896   250 copied
    20 December 1897   500   "

American edition:

    10 January 1899   500 copies

c. Edition de Luxe
                1901
    775 copies at 84/- the set.
    PLATO AND PLATONISM was no. VI of the set

    See No. 15 "Collected editions"

d. Third edition

    3 May   1901   250 copies   at 8s. 6d.

Reprints:

    22 July   1902   500 copies
    12 September 1905   500   "
     9 May   1907   500   "
    10 June   1909   500   "

American editions:
     3 May   1902   500 copies
     5 July   1902   500   "
    25 September 1903   500   "
     5 June   1905   500   "

e. New Library Edition

    30 June   1910   Printing ordered.   September 1910: Published

    1250 copies at 7s. 6d.

    See No. 16 "Collected Editions"

Title-page:

AN IMAGINARY PORTRAIT/ BY WALTER PATER [ornament]

Colophon:

Printer's ornamental device: picture of Daniel in the lions den
with words "misit Angelum Suum"/ printed by H. Daniel;/ Oxford:
1894.

Format:

Foolscap octavo $6\frac{1}{2}$" x $4\frac{1}{2}$"

Signatures:

None printed

Pagination:

[i - xii]   [1 - 4]   5 - 61   [62 - 72]

Contents:

pp. [i - viii] blanks; [ix] half-title: An/ Imaginary Portrait/
By Walter Pater/; [x - xi] blanks; [xii] 250 copies printed./
This is No.   ; [1] title-page (see above); [2] blank;
[3] fly-title: The Child in/ the House; [4] blank; 5 - 61
text; [62] small ornament; [63] blank; [64] colophon (see above)
[65 - 72] blanks

Binding:

Grey overlapping wrappers 7" x 4 7/8"; lettered in black on front
cover: An/ Imaginary Portrait/ By Walter Pater (same printing as
half-title); printing on back cover: ornament/ 1894/ ornament

Paper:

Uncut French hand-made paper

Number published and price:

250 copies at 6s. 0d.

Date of publication:

12 June 1894
(see later note on this)

. This Portrait first appeared in Macmillan's Magazine, August 1878.
(See Section I a CHRONOLOGICAL RECORD No. 26). The title then given
"Imaginary Portraits: I The Child in the House." suggests that this
was to be the first of a series.

The above volume was printed and published by Dr. C.H.O. Daniel,

AN IMAGINARY PORTRAIT

BY WALTER PATER

WILL BE SOLD
ON JUNE 12 & 13
IN WORCESTER COLLEGE GARDENS
FOR THE BENEFIT OF THE PARISH
OF S. THOMAS THE MARTYR OXFORD
AN IMAGINARY PORTRAIT by
WALTER PATER:

——THE CHILD IN THE HOUSE——

*A limited number issued—Printed in Fell
type on french hand-made paper—Price 6/.
Orders received by Mrs Daniel, Oxford.*

THE DANIEL.
PRESS

Provost of Worcester College, Oxford, on his private press. For
information regarding the Daniel Press and its owner, see The Daniel
Press: Memorials of C.H.O. Daniel with a Bibliography of the Press
1845 - 1919 (Oxford: 1921). The foreword to the book was by C.H.
Wilkinson (Worcester College); the bibliography was compiled by
F. Madan; a superb effort.

   F. Madan states that AN IMAGINARY PORTRAIT was printed "early in
May 1894". It was certainly published in June 1894. Both Provost
Daniel and his wife were on friendly terms with Pater, but the impetus
for its publication seems to have come from Mrs. Daniel. Apparently
she wished to print a short piece by Pater and an undated letter from
him suggested that "Hippolytus" was first selected and them found to
be too long (see LWP No. 265)

   Finally the Portrait was chosen, though in a letter to his friend
G. Thorne Drury dated June 17th Dr. Daniel wrote: "I have somewhat
unwillingly printed it on my wife's compulsion" (ms. The Editor). On
June 2nd 1894, Mrs Daniel wrote to Pater saying:

> "I am sending you copy No. 1 of "The Child in the House"
> "I know we have not done justice to it but we couldn't do
> "that however much we tried. It has been a very great
> "pleasure doing it, and I can never sufficiently express
> "my gratitude to you for allowing us such a treasure.   I
> "quite love,,your child.   Believe me, yours very
> "gratefully

>   Olive Daniel   (ms. Worcester College)

   On June 19th, Pater wrote to Mrs Daniel: "Many thanks for your
kind letter of June 14th.   I called at Worcester House, and found you
had taken flight for a few days: meant to have tried again today, but
am prevented by gout.   I hardly like to accept the cheque, and shall
hope to see you soon.   Meantime with sincere congratulations on the
success of the Fête,   I remain, Very truly yours,   Walter Pater.
P.S. It is a great privilege for my poor little piece to have been so
daintily attired by printer and binder." (LWP No. 269)

   The book made a somewhat unusual public appearance.   It was
issued on June 12 at a Venetian Fête and the prospectus reads:

>   Will be sold
>
>   on June 12 & 13
>
>   in Worcester College Gardens
>
>   for the benefit of the Parish
>
>   of S. Thomas the Martyr Oxford
>
>   AN IMAGINARY PORTRAIT   by
>
>   WALTER PATER:
>
>   - The Child in the House -
>
>   A limited number issued — Printed in
>   Fell type on french hand-made paper —
>   Price 6/-.   Orders received by Mrs
>   Daniel, Oxford.

The book was an instant success: "No copy was left within an hour of
the opening" (p. 133 Memorials, see above)

Pater revised this essay for the Daniel Press publication, and
Worcester College have a copy of the essay as it appeared in
Macmillan's Magazine in 1878, with the author's corrections
[Worcester College YC 12 20 (f)]. Some twenty alterations were
made, all in matters of detail and punctuation: Pater crossed out
the 'I' printed before the heading "The Child in the House"; changed
'light' to 'slight'; 'round' replaced 'about'; wrote 'his wandering
soul' for 'the wandering soul of him'; and wrote 1878 at the end. He
crossed out the 'H' of the magazine signature, leaving it "Walter
Pater". The alterations tended generally to tighten up the
expression.

In the account of the Macmillan's Magazine printing, Section I a
No. 26, will be found a note on the various publications of this
Portrait, including reference to the Pater Society of Japan and their
edition of this Portrait.

7.   GREEK STUDIES

a. First edition (posthumous)   1895

Title-page:
    GREEK STUDIES/ A SERIES OF ESSAYS/ by WALTER PATER/ late Fellow of
    Brasenose College/ Prepared for the Press/ by CHARLES L. SHADWELL/
    Fellow of Oriel College/ London/ MACMILLAN AND CO./ and New York/
    1895/ [All rights reserved]

Imprints:
    pp. [iv] and [316]: Oxford [black letter type]/ Horace Hart,
    Printer to the University

Format:
    8" x 5¼" Extra crown octavo

Signatures:
    [A]6   B - U⁸   X⁶

Pagination:
    [i - v]   vi - ix   [x - xii]   [1]2 - 315 [316]

Contents:
    p. [i] half-title: GREEK STUDIES; [ii] publisher's device: M.M.
    & Co.; tipped in leaf: recto blank, verso frontis, portrait of
    author, with tissue guard; [iii] title-page (see above); [iv]
    imprint (see above); [v] vi - ix Preface, signed C.L.S. and
    dated Oct.1894.; [x] blank; [xi] CONTENTS; [xii] blank;
    [1] 2 - 315 text; [316] imprint (see above)

Binding:
    Dark blue cloth
    Lettered in gold across spine: GREEK/ STUDIES/ WALTER/ PATER/
    MACMILLAN/ AND CO.

Number published and price:
    2,000 at 10s. 6d.

Date of publication:
    11th January 1895

        The Agreement for the publication of GREEK STUDIES was dated
13th September 1894, and signed by Hester M. Pater and Clara C. Pater.
The normal conditions were incorporated — Macmillan's to take the risk
of publication and to share profits if any equally with the Misses
Pater.   There was a further paragraph governing a ten per cent
royalty of the American retail published price per copy for every
copy sold.

        The printing was put in hand on 19th October 1894.

American edition:

    20th May 1899.   250 copies

                    _____

CONTENTS

This book contained a collection of papers, all of which had previously been published in periodicals. Titles and periodical references are given below, together with the numbers in the CHRONOLOGICAL RECORD, Section I a

---

This was a posthumous work published by Pater's friend and literary executor, Charlws Lancelot Shadwell. There is an interesting preface to the book in which Shadwell gives his reasons for publishing it, and some notes on the previous printings of each item.

> "It will, it is believed,be felt, that their value
> "is considerably enhanced by their appearance in a
> "single volume, where they can throw light upon one
> "another, and exhibit by their connexion a more complete
> "view of the scope and purpose of Mr. Pater in dealing
> "with the art and literature of the ancient world."

* There is an interesting note regarding four essays: "The Myth of Demeter and Persephone", I and II; "A Study of Dionysus" and "The Bacchanals of Euripides":

> "in 1878, Mr. Pater revised the four essays, with the intention
> "apparently, of publishing them collectively in a volume, an

"intention afterwards abandoned. The text now printed has,
"except that of "The Bacchanals", been taken from proofs then
"set up, further corrected in manuscript. "The Bacchanals",
". . . was afterwards rewritten, but with only a few
"substantial alterations, in Mr. Pater's own hand, with a view,
"probably, of republishing it with other essays. This last
"revise has been followed in the text now printed."

Pater had indeed proposed to Macmillan and Co. that a book of his
essays, including the four mentioned above, should be published (see
LWP, No. 52: 1 October 1878) under the title of 'The School of
Giorgione, and other Studies'. He changed the title in November to
Dionysus and Other Studies, but on 30 November 1878 wrote to his
publisher: "I feel more and more, as I revise the proofs of my essays,
so many inadequacies that I feel compelled, very reluntcantly, to give
up the publication of them for the present. You will of course let me
know all the cost of setting up in type, for which of course I will
immediately repay you" (LWP. No. 55). A week later he sent his cheque
for £35. for the costs.

With regard to the essays on Greek Art, the following extract from
An Oxonian Looks Back, by Lewis R. Farnell (Martin Hopkinson Ltd: 1934)
will be of interest, pp. 76-77:

"At some time in 1879 I made acquaintance with Walter Pater of
"Brasenose, in a manner that deeply influenced my life-work. He
"advertised a series of six lectures on archaic Greek art, mainly,
"I think, on the 'Chest of Kupselos' and the Aeginetan Marbles.
"This itself was an epoch in the history of Oxford studies; for
"he was the first to give this practical expression to the idea
"that Greek art was a fitting lecture subject for a classical
"teacher. To this extent, and on the Pindaric principle . . . we
"may call him the father of archaelogical teaching in Oxford,
"though his sensitive and retiring nature would have shrunk from
"being called the father of anything".

Mr. Farnell may be slightly astray with his date, but in the
Michaelmas term, 1878 Pater lectured on Mondays and Wednesdays on:
"History of Greek Art with Book I, V, VI of Pausanias" and this was
certainly a break with the regular lectures he had so far given on
Aristotle's Ethics and the Republic of Plato.

Pater left the following unfinshed manuscripts:

    "Introduction to Greek Studies"   (7 pp)

    "The Parthenon"   (16 pp)

    "Evil in Greek Art"   (10 pp)
These are at Harvard University.

The manuscript (unsigned) of the lecture of "The Marbles of Aegina"
which preceded the larger published essay, is also at Harvard

We are indeed fortunate in having records of books borrowed by
Pater from various libraries in Oxford, and the following list is taken
from the registers of the Bodleian and Brasenose College libraries:

1865	December	Stuart's Athens
1868	February	Grote. History of Greece
	November	Rawlinson. Herodotus
1871	May, July	Wyse's Peloponnisus
1872	Jan.-Mar.	Clarke's Odyssey
	Sept.-Oct.	Jowett. Dialogues of Plato.
1874	December	Newton. Halicarnassus
1875	January	Rawlinson. Venus de Milo
	July-Dec.	Paley. Euripides
	Aug.-Dec.	Claudian. Opera
	November	Custius. History of Greece
1877/8	Dec. Jan.	Scheimann. Mycenae. Troy.
1878	Aug.-Dec.	Donaldson. Pindar.
1879	March	Lessing. Lackoon
1879	Mar.-May	Miller. Literature of Greece
	July	Miller. Dorians
1882	June.Aug.	Riddell. Apology of Plato
	do.	Jowett. Thucydides
1883	May.-Oct.	Gardner. Types of Greek Coins.
1886.	March	Leake. Topography of Athens

NOTE: Many of these books were borrowed repeatedly at later
dates than those quoted.

b. <u>Edition de Luxe</u>

   1901
775 copies at 84/0 the set
<u>GREEK STUDIES</u> was Vol. VII of the set.

See No. 15: "Collected editions"

c. <u>Second edition</u>

  1901 (printed November 1900). 1000 copies

<u>Reprints:</u>

  1904 (printed December 1903)   1000 copies
  1908. 13 February   500 "

d. <u>New Library Edition</u>

  1910. 17 August (Printed) 1250 copies at 7s. 6d.
      October (Published)

8.   MISCELLANEOUS STUDIES: A SERIES OF ESSAYS

a. First edition (posthumous)   1895

Title-page:

   MISCELLANEOUS/ STUDIES/ A SERIES OF ESSAYS/ by/ WALTER PATER/ late
   Fellow of Brasenose College/ Prepared for the Press/ by/ CHARLES
   L. SHADWELL/ Fellow of Oriel College/ London/ MACMILLAN AND CO./
   and New York/ 1895/ [All rights reserved]

Imprints:

   pp. [iv] and [260]: OXFORD (black letter type)/ Horace Hart,
   Printer to the University

Format:

   Extra Crown Octavo   8" x 5 3/8"

Signatures:

   [A]^8 B - R^8 S^2

Pagination:

   [i - v]   vi - xiv   [xv - xvi]   [1] 2 - 259 [260]

Contents:

   p. [i] half-title: MISCELLANEOUS STUDIES; [ii] publisher's
   monogram consisting of intertwined M.M. & Co.; [iii] title-page
   (see above0; [iv] imprint (see above); [v] vi - xiv Preface,
   signed C.L.S. and dated August 1895.; [xv] CONTENTS; [xvi] blank;
   [1] 2 - 259 text; [260] imprint (see above0

Binding:
   Dark-blue cloth
   Lettered in gold across spine: MISCELLANEOUS/ STUDIES/ WALTER/
   PATER/ MACMILLAN/ AND CO.

Number published and price:

   1,500 copies at 9s.

Date of publication:

   18th October 1895
   Printing ordered 20th June 1895

Reprints:

   29 June   1898   250 copies
   29 November 1898/
                  1899   250 copies
   14 September 1900   500 copies

American editions:

   14 July   1900   500 copies
   21 October 1902   500 copies

                         _____

                            101

CONTENTS:

This book contains a collection of papers, most of which had
previously been published in periodicals. Titles and periodical
references are given below, together with the number in the
CHRONOLOGICAL RECORD, Section I a

    In his Preface to the book, Shadwell wrote:
    "It is with some hesitation that the paper
    "on Diaphaneitè, the last in this volume,
    "has been added, as the only specimen known
    "to be preserved of those early essays of
    "Mr. Pater's, by which his literary gifts
    "were first made known to the small circle
    "of his Oxford friends"

    Shadwell followed Pater in his placement of the
    grave accent in the title.

The Preface to this book contains "a brief chronological list" of Pater's writings. This is defective and omits many of Pater's essays and reviews.

----

b. Edition de Luxe

   1901
775 copies at 84/- the set

MISCELLANEOUS STUDIES was Vol. VIII of the set

See No. 15: "Collected editions"

c. Second edition:

  9 June   1904   500 copies

Reprints:

 5 November 1906/
         1907   500 copies
10 June 1909   500   "

American editions:

 6 February 1905   500 copies
23 April   1907   500   "

d. New Library Edition

17 August 1910   1250 copies at 7s. 6d.   Published Nov. 1910.

See No. 16 "Collected editions"

9.   GASTON DE LATOUR: AN UNFINISHED ROMANCE

a. **First edition** (posthumous)   1896

Title-page:
GASTON DE LATOUR/ AN UNFINISHED ROMANCE/ by /WALTER PATER/ late
Fellow of Brasenose College/ Prepared for the Press by/ CHARLES
L. SHADWELL/ Fellow of Oriel College/ LONDON [black letter type]/
MACMILLAN AND CO. Ltd./ New York: The Macmillan Co./ 1896/ [All
rights reserved]

Imprints:
pp. [iv]:Oxford [black letter type]/ Horace Hart, Printer to the
University; 200: Oxford: Horace Hart, Printer to the University.

Format:
Extra crown octavo   8" x 5 3/8"

Signatures:
[a]^6 B - N^8 O^4

Pagination:
[1 - 2]   [i - v] vi - vii [viii - x]   [1] 2 - 200

Contents:
pp. [1 - 2] blanks; [i] half title: GASTON DE LATOUR; [ii]
Publisher's monogram consisting of M. M. & Co. intertwined; [iii]
title-page (see above); [iv] imprint (see above); [v] vi - vii
Preface signed C.L.S. and dated July 1896.; [viii] blank; [ix]
CONTENTS; [x] blank; [1] 2 - 200 text with imprint (see
above) on p. 200

Binding:
Dark blue cloth
Lettered in gold across spine: GASTON/ DE/ LATOUR/ WALTER/ PATER/
MACMILLAN/ AND CO.

Number published and price:
1,500 copies at 7s. 6d.

Date published:
6 October 1896
(Printed 20 July 1896)

Reprint:
14 January 1897   500 copies

CONTENTS:
Six chapters had prior periodical printings, the other was prepared
from a manuscript left by Pater. Details are given below, with

references to Section I a CHRONOLOGICAL RECORD.

The following news item was printed in the Athenaeum (No. 3050,
April 10th 1886, p. 490):
    "Mr. Walter Pater is at work upon a new romance of the past.
    "This time the scene will be laid in the sixteenth century and
    "in France; but the work will not be finished for some time."
The note was provided by Pater's friend, William Sharp.

    On 25th August 1890, Miss Katherine Bradley (Michael Field) wrote
"Pater is going to forswear a holiday to finish Gaston de la Tour —
a longer book than Marius".   (Works and Days: John Murray: 1933) p.
119.

    On 22nd January (1892) Pater wrote to William Canton: " . . .
having some other works near completion, viz. a second series of
Imaginary Portraits and Gaston de Latour, a sort of Marius in France,
in the 16th century.   Parts of this were published in Macmillan's
Magazine some years ago."   (LWP No. 242)

PATER'S READING:

Pater owned a copy of Ronsard's Oeuvres Completes(1857) and this was found in his library (in a very handsome bookcase) after his death.

Brasenose College Library have a record of Pater borrowing Montaigne's Essays in the Autumn of 1877.

---

b. Edition de Luxe

1900
775 copies at 84/- the set
GASTON DE LATOURwas in Volume IV, together with IMAGINARY PORTRAITS
See No. 15: "Collected editions"

c. Second edition:

16 September 1902   500 copies   at 7s. 6d.

Reprinted:

12 June 1907   500 copies

d. New Library Edition:

26 May 1910.   1250 copies at 7s. 6d.   (Pubkished Dec. 1910)
See No. 16: "Collected editions"

e. Thomas Bird Mosher (Portland , Maine, U.S.A.) published GASTON DE LATOUR in a 12mo volume of x + 130 pages in his Old World Series. This was a limited edition of 925 copies, printed on Van Gelder paper. with 50 copies on Japan vellum. There was an introduction by William Marion Reedy.

THE MANUSCRIPTS

1. Harvard University: fragments.

2. The Berg Collection, The New York Public Library.
      Chapters I — V and VII (published)

3. Mr. John Sparrow, Warden of All Souls College, Oxford.
      Chapters VIII — XIII (unpublished)

1. In January 1961 The Houghton Library, Harvard University, Cambridge, Massachusetts, U.S.A. purchased several hundred quarto sheets of unpublished manuscripts left by Walter Pater (for a full listing of these 'fragments' see Section II Unpublished Writings: b. MANUSCRIPTS).   One such manuscript is listed by the Library as follows:

        [Gaston de Latour]
        A.MS (unsigned); [n.p., n.d.] 13s. (16p.)
        Comprises: a fragment of ch. 8, a fragment of ch. 12,
      a leaf of notes, and ch. 13, the last evidently in the
      autograph of Clara Pater.

2. The manuscripts of Chapters I - V and VII of the book, GASTON DE LATOUR are in the Berg Collection, New York Public Library, N.Y. Unfortunately the manuscript of Chapter VI "Shadow of Events", printed by Pater's executors from manuscript left by him is lost, and all efforts to locate it have failed. The N.Y.P.L. holding was obtained, through a Chicago bookseller from a private person in England, who had no connection with Pater or his family and is unlikely to have any other manuscripts of Pater.

Mrs Lola L. Szladits, Curator of the Collection, kindly informs me: "The manuscript of Pater's Gaston de Latour is 276 pages long, written on lined quarto sheets on one side of a sheet. Although some pages are rather heavily marked up, I would say that on the whole the ms. is best described as lightly corrected and revised."

The New York Public Library Bulletin, Vol. 63, April 1959, p. 208, describing its recent acquisition makes the comment: "The manuscript of Chapters I - V and of Chapter VII is shown here. It displays differences from the printed text. It is particularly noteworthy that Pater seems to have disregarded his corrections in the manuscript and to have published his first thoughts."

3. As stated above, the manuscript of the unpublished chapters of GASTON DE LATOUR are in the possession of Mr. John Sparrow, All Souls College, Oxford. Mr. Sparrow has made a typed copy of "The Unpublished Chapters of Gaston de Latour" with listed contents as follows:

Ch.	VIII	An empty house	p. 1
	IX	A Poison-Daisy	6
	X	Anteros	12
	XI	. . . . .	21
	XII	A Wedding	32
		Book III	
	XIII	Mi-Careme	34

The manuscript is mainly on quarto off-white paper. It is faintly ruled paper with the right-hand edge uncut, sometimes it is so on the left hand. I get the impression that the paper has been taken from a bound book.

Pater numbered the leaves (he wrote on one side only) for the most part with a bold clear figure in the top right hand corner (Arabic not Roman figures). The figures are not for the book, but start again with each chapter. The total number of pages is 164

Pater wrote on one side of the paper only and on alternate lines. The black ink has survived well.

The writing is good, clear and incisive. Towards the end of the manuscript the writing is not as clear or good as in the earlier stages Then it seems more hurried, the pages are more fragmentary, and it might well be that the earlier pages of the manuscript represent a second writing. I except Ch. XII "A Wedding" which has several pages of writing which seem draft only, yet I cannot think that they are a first draft. Later chapters, say "Mi-Careme" may represent earlier states of draft. One cannot be dogmatic as it may be that some parts came easier and therefore look to be a second state.

In addition, there are a number of small rectangular slips of writing, 4" x 2". Some are loose, some stuck on by stamp edging to the page in which they should be inserted. The slips seem to be cut out or torn from larger pieces of paper. Odd ones seem to be from his favourite blue-tinged letter paper.

Pater left considerable blanks on some pages. Sometimes several versions of a word or phrase are given without erasure to indicate the final choice; sometimes the original is erased and the second choice left above.

10.   ESSAYS FROM THE "GUARDIAN"

a. <u>First (privately printed) edition</u>   1896

<u>Title-page:</u>

    ESSAYS [in red]/ from/ THE "GUARDIAN"/ by/ WALTER PATER/ late
    Fellow of Brasenose College/ LONDON/ PRINTED FOR PRIVATE
    CIRCULATION[in red]/ at the Chiswick Press/ 1896

<u>Imprint:</u>

    p. [164]: Publisher's Device (Anchor and Line)/ Chiswick Press:-
    Charles Whittingham & Co./ Tooks Court, Chancery Lane, London

<u>Format:</u>

    Crown octavo   7" x 4 3/8"

<u>Signatures:</u>

    [A]^4 B - L^8 M^2

<u>Pagination:</u>

    [i - v[vi   [vii - viii] [1 - 3] 4 - 163 [164]

<u>Contents:</u>

    P. [i] half-title:Ornament/ ESSAYS FROM THE/ "GUARDIAN"/ Ornament
    [ii] Only 100 copies printed, of which this is/ No.   ; [iii]
    title-page (see above0; [iv] blank; [v] - vi Preface with
    ornaments at head of [v] and end of vi; [vii] Contents with
    ornaments at head and foot; [viii] blank; [1] divisional-title:
    I./ ENGLISH LITERATURE./ February 17th, 1886./ ornament; [2]
    blank; [3] 4 - 163 Text [ornaments at head and end of each item];
    [164] imprint (see above)

<u>Binding:</u>

    Blue-grey boards
    Paper label on spine: ESSAYS/ FROM THE/ GUARDIAN/ ——— / by/
    WALTER/ PATER
    Paper: hand made Van Gelder paper, uncut

<u>Number published and price:</u>

    100 copies at £7. 10s.

<u>Date published:</u>
    6 October 1896

<u>CONTENTS:</u>

    These are given in the order of the book. The short-title of the
book is followed by the fuller title at the head of each review in the
text.   The numbers in the CHRONOLOGICAL RECORD, Section I a are given.

The impetus for the publication of this book came from Edmund Gosse a friend of Pater, and one who was persona grata with Hester Maria and Clara Ann Pater. They agreed to his publishing the book in a letter which is quoted below:

June 24 1896

"We do not see any reason why you should not do as you propose about the

110

ESSAYS

FROM

THE "GUARDIAN"

BY

WALTER PATER

LATE FELLOW OF BRAZENOSE COLLEGE

LONDON

PRINTED FOR PRIVATE CIRCULATION

AT THE CHISWICK PRESS

1896

"essays in the 'Guardian.' They would make a pretty little booklet &
"interest his admirers, & I do not think he would have liked them
"published in any more formal manner, as he would have written them
"with less care than more important things. As you say, a private
"edition would not affect the interests of his publishers, even if
"later any more fragments should be published, which however we do not
"intend at present. With kind regards, Yours very sincerely

(signed) Clara Pater"

In his Preface to the book, Gosse stated: "It has been discovered
through the kindness of the present editor of the "Guardian," Mr. D.C.
Lathbury, that Walter Pater contributed to the pages of that newspaper
nine anonymous articles.. So distinguished an interest attaches to
everything which proceeded from the fastisious pen of the great critic
that it has been thought worth while to preserve these nine essays,
although their positive value may be slight. . . "   (It was however
well known at the time that Pater was writing for the Guardian)

After publication, Hester Pater wrote to Gosse on November 9th
1896: "The articles make a sweet little book, the binding is most
charming, I should think people will like to have it."

b. American edition   1897

In 1897 a pious facsimile of the 1896 edition was published by
Thomas Bird Mosher. It was printed by the Thurston Print, Exchange
Street, Portland, Maine, USA, and published by Mosher at 45 Exchange
Street, Portland Maine. It comprised xiv + 164 pages with a portrait
of Pater as a frontispiece (a copy of the Rothenstein sketch). It was
a limited edition of 400 copies, printed on Van Gelder hand-made paper
and 5o numbered copies on Japan vellum. Though of limited issue, it
must rank as the first public edition.

Mosher published a second edition in 1898.

So carefully was this facsimile printed that even the ornaments were
copied and binding, paper and title label were also identical. Mosher
was indeed entitled to claim that "Our reprint, short of absolute
photographic reproduction, is in facsimile, as far as type, paper and
binding can make it." In his introductory note he also listed eleven
uncollected articles by Pater which had been cited in the Athenaeum,
June 12, 1897 by Arthur Symons, which in 1903 he published in
UNCOLLECTED ESSAYS (1903) (See No. 11 of this Section)

c. First English Public edition   1901

In Sept 1901 Macmillan and Co. published their first printing of
ESSAYS FROM THE 'GUARDIAN' as an extra volume to their Collected
edition of Pater's works: the Edition de Luxe (see No. 15 of this
Section). Though not numbered as part of the set it was identical in
production with the other volumes. A description is given below:

<u>Title-page</u>

ESSAYS [in red]/ from/ 'THE GUARDIAN' [in red]/ by/ WALTER PATER/ Fellow of Brasenose College/ LONDON/ MACMILLAN AND CO. Limited [in red]/ New York: The Macmillan Company/ 1901/ <u>All rights reserved</u>

<u>Imprint</u>:

p. [149]: <u>Printed by</u> R. & R. Clark, Limited, <u>Edinburgh</u>

<u>Format</u>:

Medium octavo   9" x 6"

<u>Signatures</u>:

[A]^4 B - K^8 L^4

<u>Pagination</u>:

[i - viii]   1 [2]   3 - 148   [149 - 152]

<u>Contents</u>:

p. [i] half-title: ESSAYS FROM 'THE GUARDIAN'; [ii] Publisher's monogram: M.M. & Co. intertwined; [iii] title-page (see above); [iv] blank;[v]NOTE/ The nine papers contained in the following/ volume originally appeared anonymously in/ The Guardian newspaper. ; [vi] blank; [vii] CONTENTS; [viii]blank; 1 divisional title: I/ ENGLISH LITERATURE/ 17th February 1886; 2 blank; 3 - 148 [149] text with imprint (see above) on p. [149]; [150 - 152] blanks

<u>Binding</u>:

Boards covered with green silk; medallion in centre of front cover; highly decorated spine in gold with acanthus leaf motif Lettering across spine: THE/ WORKS OF/ WALTER/ PATER/ESSAYS./ FROM.THE/ GUARDIAN/ MACMILLAN & CO.

<u>Number published and price</u>:

775 copies at 8s. 6d.

<u>Date published</u>:

4th September 1901

The following note in the <u>Academy</u>, Vol. LXI, No. 1531, 7th Sept., 1901, p. 183, is of interest:

The Literary Week

"The handsomest and most interesting book that the "week has brought us is Messrs. Macmillan's issue "of Walter Pater's "Essays from the Guardian". The "delicate green cover and gold acanthus design, are, "of course, uniform with the complete "Edition de "Luxe" issued by the same publisher. The volume "consists of nine papers, which originally appeared "anonymously.

When in 1900 the Misses Pater were approached by Macmillan's
regarding the Edition de Luxe of Pater's works, Hester Pater, giving
their consent (January 25th: ms. Macmillan and Co.) went on to say:
"With regard to the Reviews from the Guardian we would rather not have
these included, as they were never revised or intended for further
publication." I have no information of the reasons for the change of
heart by Pater's sisters.

A mild public controversy ensued upon the publication of the 1901
volume, some literary people considering that it should not have had a
public issue. Arthur Symons wrote a letter to the Athenaeum, No. 3856,
September 21, 1901, in which he contended that the earlier privately
printed volume had only been intended for the inner circle of Pater's
friends: "it was as if a copy of a private letter had been handed
about among friends, who could be relied upon to take it for what it
was. But they were never part of Mr. Pater's 'Works', and they should
not have been offered to the public under that title . . . To print as
part of his 'Works' a quite arbitrary selection from his literary
journalism is to do a serious wrong to a writer who is no longer able
to defend himself against either his enemies or his friends."

In the next issue of the Athenaeum, No. 3857, September 28, 1901,
F.M. Bourdillon wrote defending the publication. He contended that
once the essays had been published, even in a private edition, further
publication was bound to take place. "There must be many like myself
who, having failed to be one of the lucky hundred of the "inner circle",
are very glad to possess this reprint. Plainly it was impossible for a
publisher who was trying to issue Pater's works in a complete form to
leave out these essays, though he might and doubtless would have done so
had they remained as mere uncollected reviews in the files of the
Guardian." There was a reply from Symons in the Oct. 5 issue, No.
3858, p. 453, and Bourdillon had the last word on Oct. 12, No. 3859.

Reprints:

    13 August 1901 (printed). Published September.   500 copies

     9 June   1903 (extra crown octavo)   500   "

     2 August 1906   -do.-   500

d. New Library Edition:

    26 May 1910   1250 copies at 7s. 6d.

    See No. 16: "Collected editions"

Title-page:

UNCOLLECTED ESSAYS/ By/WALTER PATER/ [Publisher's Device in red]/
Printed for Thomas B. Mosher and/ Published by him at 45 Exchange/
Street Portland Maine MDCCCCIII

Imprint:

p. [162]: Printed by Smith & Sale/ Exchange Street, Portland,
Maine, U.S.A.

Signatures:

None printed but makes up as follows:
A^4 B - L^8 M^4

Pagination:

[i - v]   vi   [vii - viii]   [1 - 3]   4 - 161   [162 - 168]

Contents:

p. [i] half-title: Ornamental border/ UNCOLLECTED/ ESSAYS/
Ornaments; [ii] 450 copies of this book have/ been printed on Van
Gelder hand-made paper and the type distributed.; [iii] title-page
(see above); [iv] blank; [v] - vi NOTE (with ornamental border
above [v] and ornaments at end [vi]); [vii] CONTENTS (with
ornamental border above and ornaments at end); [viii] blank;
[1] divisional title: I/ SYMONDS'S "RENAISSANCE IN ITALY"/ The
Academy, July 31, 1875; [2] blank; [3] 4 - 161 text; [162]
imprint (see above); [163 - 168] blanks

Divisional titles throughout

Binding:

Blue-grey boards
Paper label on spine: UNCOL-/LECTED/ ESSAYS/ ———/ by/ WALTER/
PATER
Uncut hand-made Van Gelder paper

CONTENTS:

These are given in the order in which they appear in the book.
Together with the titles are given the periodical details and the
numbers in the Chronological Record in Section I a

Sectiom I a

1. Symonds's "Renaissance in Italy"   19
        "Renaissance in Italy: The Age of Despots"
        By John Addington Symonds (London: Smith Elder
        & Co. 1875) Academy, July 31, 1875

UNCOLLECTED ESSAYS
BY WALTER PATER

PRINTED FOR THOMAS B. MOSHER AND
PUBLISHED BY HIM AT 45 EXCHANGE
STREET PORTLAND MAINE MDCCCCIII

The publications of Thomas Bird Mosher must bulk large in any comprehensive account of Walter Pater's writings.   A brief biographical sketch of this prince of pirates together with a list of his Pater extracts and other publications will be found in Appendix a : Thomas Bird Mosher - Man of Letters

Title-page:

    SKETCHES AND REVIEWS/ BY WALTER PATER/ Ornament: a Penguin with
    "The Penguin Series"/ NEW YORK/ BONI AND LIVERIGHT/ 1919

Imprint:

    None given

Format:

    Duodecimo (Library of Congress catalogue) 7 3/8" x 4 3/8"

Signatures:

    None given

Pagination:

    [i - v]   vi   [vii - x]   1 - 150

Contents:

    p. [i] half-title: SKETCHES AND REVIEWS; [ii] blank; [iii]
    title-page (see above); [iv]: Copyright 1919/ By BONI & LIVERIGHT
    Inc. Printed in the U.S.A.; [v] - vi Foreword, signed Albert
    Mordell, Philadelphia, 1919; [viii] CONTENTS; [viii] blank; [ix]
    fly-title: SKETCHES AND REVIEWS; [x] blank; 1 - 150 text

Binding:

    Yellow boards with parchment spine
    On front cover in black: SKETCHES AND/ REVIEWS/ by WALTER PATER/
    ornament BONI AND LIVERIGHT/ NEW YORK . Title surrounded with
    double black lined frame with ornaments in each corner.
    On spine in black: SKETCHES/ AND/ REVIEWS/ ——— / WALTER/ PATER/
    ornament: A Penguin "The Penguin Series" underneath/ Boni and
    Liveright

Published price:

    $1.25

Date of Publication:

    March 1919

CONTENTS:

    These are given in the order of the book. Together with the title
will be found details of the periodical printing and, where applicable,
the publication in UNCOLLECTED ESSAYS. The number of each item in the
CHRONOLOGICAL RECORD Section 1 a is also given

1. Aesthetic Poetry

     This was first printed as the first part of a
     review of "Poems of William Morris" in the
     Westminster Review, October 1868. It was
     later printed in APPRECIATIONS (first edition)
     1889, but Mordell included it in SKETCHES AND
     REVIEWS because Pater omitted it from the
     second edition.

2. M. le Maitre's "Serenus and other Tales"   50
     Macmillan's Magazine, November 1887
     Uncollected Essays 1903, p. 13

3. The Life and Letters of Gustave Flaubert   59
     Pall Mall Gazette, 25 August 1888
     Uncollected Essays 1903, p. 49

4. "Correspondance of Gustave Flaubert"   68
     Athenaeum 3 August 1889
     Uncollected Essays 1903, p. 101

5. Coleridge as a Theologian   4
     This title was Mordell's own. He printed
     those parts of the Westminster Review,
     Jan 1866 review, "Coleridge's Writings"
     which Pater omitted from "Coleridge" in
     APPRECIATIONS, 1889

6. Wordsworth   61
     Athenaeum 26 January 1889
     Uncollected Essays 1903, p. 65

7. A Novel by Mr. Oscar Wilde   79
     The Bookman, November 1891
     Uncollected Essays, 1903, p. 123

8. A Poet with Something to Say   63
     Pall Mall Gazette 23 March 1889
     Uncollected Essays 1903, p. 77

9. Mr. George Moore as an Art Critic   88
     Daily Chronicle, 10 June 1893
     Uncollected Essays 1903, p. 135

CIRCUMSTANCES OF PUBLICATION

     This book was published by Boni and Liveright, New York, in 1919.
The company is now reincorporated as "The Liveright Publishing
Corporation."

     Mr. Mordell in his Preface stated: "This volume is the first
collection in book form of nearly all the known fugitive writings of
Walter Pater." Actually seven out of the nine papers had appeared in

Thomas B. Mosher's UNCOLLECTED ESSAYS (1903), only "Coleridge as a
Theologian" and "Aesthetic Poetry" not being in the earlier book.
Forty-three years after the publication of his book, Mr. Mordell told
me that he had been aware of the Mosher limited edition and had seen
it years before, but it had temporarily slipped his mind and "I called
my book the first collection when I should have said the first trade
collection, first popular edition. But Mosher did not have the
Coleridge."

Albert Mordell: Man of Literature

Albert Mordell was born on August 13th 1885, the year in which
Marius the Epicurean was published, in Philadelphia, USA. He was the
elder son of Jewish parents, who came from Lithuania in the eighties.
The father, who earned the family bread by teaching Hebrew, was indeed
a bookman, an authority on Biblical grammar, and published articles
and books on linguistics and the Hebrew Classics.

Albert was destined by his father to be a Hebrew scholar, but the
boy himself had ambitions in the wider world of iterature. After
leaving Central High School he decided to earn a living by law, but
spent days and nights at the library designing a history of English
literature and writing poems in imitation of Tennyson. These projects
were abandoned the day he discovered the poetry of Walt Whitman "
all my plans for writing academic literature vanished." He attempted
poems in the Whitman vein, and made the acquaintance of Horace Traubel
Whitman's foremost disciple. Under this new influence, he renounced
law and tried to earn a living as a newspaper reported, writing for
the Philadelphia Public Ledger.

Shortly before his 21st birthday, Mordell left Philadelphia
resolved on a writer's career in New York, reaching the capital in
July 1906 with $12, borrowed,in his pocket. The next twelve months
were a mortifying experience. He moved from room to room, unable to
pay the rent, and within a year had to return to Philadelphia. He
nursed his misery in the City libraries, earned some money by tutoring,
and finally in 1910 passed a State examination and was admitted to the
Philadelphia bar.

From then until his death he conducted a flourishing legal
business but never lost his love for literature. His first large
lawyer's fee went to a printer to publish his first and favourite
book: The Shifting of Literary Values, in which he pleaded for the
right of each generation to choose its own classics. The book
received international attention and was greeted as a splendid
undertaking by writers such as Galsworthy, Georg Brandes and Havelock
Ellis.

In January 1913 he started writing for Philadelphia journals a
series of interviews with celebrated foreign and American celebrities.
He interviewed William Jennings Bryan, the Nebraska statesman and
amateur theologian; Louis Untermeyer, poet and anthologist; Fannie
Hirst, that artist in the distillation of lacrymae Americanae; Padraic
Colum, the Irish Poet; Hilda Doolittle, writer of Imagist verse; a
number of people who had known Walt Whitman well; and Count Ilya

Tolstoy, son of the noveslist.

For a long time he spent his gifts on the scholarly resurrection of writings by great artists which had undergone dusty oblivion in the files of old journals and magazines. He spent years in collecting and editing buried essays of Lafcadio Hearn and in 1918 published his first collection of Hearn's 'lost' essays and stories, Karma.

He did yeoman service to the work of Henry James, exhuming many stories which had received decent burial in the Atlantic Monthly and other periodicals.

Mordell became interested in the mysteries of pschoanalysis and became a convert to the Freudian theories. He coupled his psychology with literary criticism and in 1919 (a prolific year) published his most famous book The Erotic Motive in Literature which brought him fame and which was reissued in paper back garb in 1963.

His biography of Whittier, published in 1933, was the result of two years hard labour among the archives of several States and this became the definitive biography. The measure of Mordell's achievements in the scale of public opinion was his assignment to write the articles on the New England liberator-bard in the Encyclopaedia Britannica and the Dictionary of American Biography.

The Chant
of the
Celestial Sailors

an unpublished poem by

WALTER PATER

Thirty copies printed by E. H. BLAKENEY
at his private press, 1928

Title-page:

THE CHANT/ OF THE/ CELESTIAL SAILORS [three lines of title in black letter type]/ an unpublished poem by/ WALTER PATER/ Thirty copies printed by E.H. BLAKENEY/ at his private press, 1928

Signatures:

None given: the booklet, apart from its cover, consists of six leaves, stitched in the centre

Pagination:

Pages not numbered [xii]

Format:

7½" x 5"

Contents:

p. [i] half title: THE CHANT OF THE/ CELESTIAL SAILORS; [ii] blank; [iii] title-page (see above); [iv] blank; [v vii ix] text; [vi viii x xii] blanks; [xi] NOTE. — The first part of this poem was written last./ "It describes rather his waning ideas of heavenly/ progress."

Binding:

Stiff brown card covers
Title in black on front cover: THE CHANT OF THE/ CELESTIAL SAILORS
The British Museum copy has gold lettering on the cover.

Date of publication:

March 1928

This poem was printed and published by Edward Henry Blakeney, M.A., on his private press at Winchester College, where he was then a master. The only other item concerning Pater he printed was also a poem: INSCRIPTION FOR THE LIFE OF WALTER PATER, also in 1928. See No. 14 in this section.

I have not been able to discover the nature of Blakeney's interest in Pater. I have however seen an extract from a letter from him to a poet to whom he had written for permission to print some poems and from that letter it appears that he sometimes printed items for the benefit of boys at Winchester College.

I suspect that he saw a copy of the poem which was owned by Pater's boyhood friend, John Rainier McQueen, as the latter's manuscript also has the note printed on Pater's 'waning ideas of heavenly progress'. That note was made by another of Pater's friends, Rev. M.B. Moorhouse.

An account of Pater's early poetry, copies of which have survived in manuscript, will be found in Section II Unpublished Writings - c POETRY.

<u>E.H. BLAKENEY and his Private Press</u>

Edward Henry Blakeney was born on 15th August 1869. He went to Westminster School, gained an exhibition to Trinity College, Cambridge, where he took his B.A. degree in 1891 and M.A. in 1895. He gained the post of Head Master of Sandwich Grammar School in 1895, an early age for such a post ! He ta.ught at a number of schools, besides Winchester, and for a time (1929-1931) was a lecturer in English Literature at University College, Southampton. He published several books of original poems of his own composition, and also translated Homer's <u>Iliad</u>, Horace <u>De Arte Poetica</u>, Plato's <u>Apology</u> and other classical works. He edited "Peaks, Passes and Glaciers" 1926; Bacon's <u>Essays</u>; Milton's <u>Paradise Regained</u>; Everyman's <u>Classical Dictionary</u>; and was the proprietor of the Scholastic Press. He married in 1895. He was on the staff of Winchester College from 1918 to 1830 and again for a term in 1932. He retired to Winchester where he died in 1954.

Information on Blakeney's printing activities can be found in G.S. Tomkinson. <u>A Select Bibliography of Modern Presses</u> (First Edition Club: 1928) and Will Ransom. <u>Private Presses and their books</u> (New York: 1929). Tomkinson gives a List of Books Printed at the Blakeney Press which gives details of 14 books commencing with <u>A Death on the Prairie</u>. A poem by Edward Henry Blakeney. 1909 and concluding with another book of verses by the printer <u>In the Vale of Tears</u> 1926. I have a list of 30 later books printed by Blakeney, and in view of the interest now taken in private press printing I give them in short title form below, together with the numbers printed:

Year	Title and Size		No. of copies
1927	Song of Deborah	$7\frac{1}{2}$ x 5	30
	Mountain Memories	$7\frac{1}{2}$ x 5	30
	Shelley: the Celandine	$7\frac{1}{2}$ x 5	30
	Shelley: trans. from Greek Anthology	6 x $4\frac{1}{2}$	30
1928	Walter Pater: poem		30
	Walter Pater: Inscription		14
	Four Gnostic Hymns translated	$7\frac{1}{2}$ x 5	--
1929	W.S. Landor: a letter	$7\frac{1}{2}$ x 5	20
	Edmund Gosse: two poems	$4\frac{1}{2}$ x 6	14
1930	Austin Dobson: three poems	$7\frac{1}{2}$ x 5	25
	Siegfried Sassoon: a Sonnet	$8\frac{1}{2}$ x $6\frac{1}{2}$	14
	George Gissing: a Poem	$7\frac{1}{2}$ x $5\frac{1}{2}$	16
1932	Memories, by Rudyard Kipling	$7\frac{1}{2}$ x $5\frac{1}{2}$	15
1933	Tiberianus: 'annisibat'	9 x 6	15
1936	John Masefield: to R.K.	6 x $4\frac{1}{2}$	--
	Shelley: a letter	9 x 6	14
	Hood: a sonnet	6 x $4\frac{1}{2}$	15
	Alfred Noyes: poem	$6\frac{3}{4}$ x $8\frac{1}{2}$	--
1937	" " 'Youth and memory' (poem)	6 x $4\frac{1}{2}$	30

1938	Alfred Noyes: 'Wizards' (poem)	$6\frac{3}{4}$ x $6\frac{1}{2}$	15
1936	Geo. Meredith (a letter)	$7\frac{1}{2}$ x 5	--
1939	Alf. Noyes: 'the dead Pope speaks' a poem	$4\frac{1}{2}$ x 6	--
1940	R. Bridges (a verse parody)	6 x $4\frac{1}{2}$	9
	Unpublished letters to Alfred Noyes from Swinburne, Barry Pain; two other letters from (1)Robert Browning (2) Mazzini	7 x $4\frac{1}{2}$	25
	Rooseveldt (President): letter to A. Noyes	9 x 6	36

The following books are collections of verses by the Author-Printer. Not more than 65 copies were printed of any volume

1926	In the Vale of Years	7 x $5\frac{1}{2}$	Garamond
1929	Alpine Poems	$8\frac{1}{2}$ x $6\frac{1}{2}$	Baskerville type type 14 pt
1933	Falling leaves	$8\frac{1}{2}$ x $6\frac{1}{2}$	do.
1937	Occasional Verses	6 x $4\frac{1}{2}$	Baskerville 12 pt.
1939	At the Day's End	$8\frac{1}{2}$ x $6\frac{1}{2}$	do. 14 pt

The papers used were mainly Old Drury, sometimes de la Rue, handmade. Paper wrappers on plain boards with labels.

The hand press is a Phoenix, of German make.

Blakeney was certainly a man of probounced literary tastes. He kept in touch with men of letters and obtained permission to print samples of their work. Some of his books are unique first editions of newly discovered pieces, notably two poems by Shelley (Will Ransom).

He had many diverse activities - artist craftsman; poet; teacher; translater; literary amateur - all of which interlocked shrewdly.

Types employed:

Garamond: 12pt. 10pt. 18pt

Baskerville: 12 pt 14 pt (apart from titlings)

Device: a phoenix, from a drawing by R.M. Gleadowe

Bookplate: from Woodblock by the late F. Unwin.

Title-page:

> INSCRIPTION/ FOR THE LIFE OF WALTER PATER/ TO THE READER

Colophon:

> p. ⌊iii⌋: These Pleasant Lines (from some old author/unknown to
> us) were inserted by Pater in/ front of a book of MS Poems begun
> in March/ 1859.   They were first printed in April 1928/ by E.H.
> Blakeney at his Private Press, Win/chester, in 13 pt. Baskerville
> cast by/ Messrs Stephenson & Blake

Size:

> 8 x 6¼ in.

The book consists of four leaves stitched in the centre

Contents:

> ⌊ i ⌋ title-page (see above); ⌊ii⌋ blank; ⌊iii⌋ text; ⌊iv⌋blank
> ⌊ v ⌋ text ; ⌊vi⌋ blank; ⌊vii - viii⌋ blanks

No statement of the number printed appears in this booklet, but
Blakeney gives it as 14 in a list he prepared of his publications.

This poem was printed on p. ⌊vi⌋ of volume I of Thomas Wright's
Life of Walter Pater (1907), and, as Blakeney's printing is an exact
reproduction of Wright's quotation, it is presumed that the Life was
the source.   Wright, in a footnote to the poem, partially reprinted
by Blakeney (see Colophon above) stated: "These pleasant lines from
some old English author whose name we have not been able to trace, were
inserted by Walter Pater in front of a book of manuscript poems
commenced in March 1859 . . . "

No outside source for this poem has yet been found.   The wording
and style are not unlike poems which Pater was writing at the time and
there is therefore a presumption that this was composed by him.

A biographical note on E.H. Blakeney, together with a list of
books printed by him will be found in the previous item No. 13:
THE CHANT OF THE CELESTIAL SAILORS

15. EDITION DE LUXE   1900/1901

This is the first of two collected editions of Walter Pater's
works (the other being No. 16: New Library Edition: 1910).   It
comprises eight volumes, with an additional volume, similar in format,
for ESSAYS FROM 'THE GUARDIAN'

A full description is given of Volume I, in order to illustrate
the set, the remaining volumes being listed with any distinctive
details.

I.   THE RENAISSANCE: STUDIES IN ART AND POETRY

Title-page:

THE RENAISSANCE ⌊in red⌋/ STUDIES IN ART AND POETRY/ by/ WALTER
PATER/ Fellow of Brasenose College/ LONDON/ MACMILLAN AND CO.
Limited ⌊in red⌋/ New York: The Macmillan Company/ 1900/ All
rights reserved

Imprint:

p. ⌊239⌋: Printed by R. & R. Clark, Limited, Edinburgh.

Format:

Medium octavo   9" x 6"

Signatures:

[a]¹   [A]⁸   B - Q⁸

Pagination:

[i - vi]   vii - xv   [xvi - xviii]   1 - 238 ⌊239-240⌋

Contents:

p. [i] edition notice and half-title: The Works/ of/ WALTER
PATER [in red]/ in eight volumes/ I/ THE RENAISSANCE; [ii]
publisher's monogram consisting of M.M. & Co. intertwined;
vignette in red tipped in with tissue guard; [iii] title-page (see
above); [iv] This Edition consists of Seven Hundred and Seventy-
five Copies; ⌊v ⌋ Dedication/ ──── / to/ C.L.S./ February 1873./
⌊vi⌋ blank; vii-xv Preface; ⌊xvi⌋ blank; ⌊xvii⌋ CONTENTS;
⌊xviii⌋ blank; 1 - 238 ⌊239⌋ text with imprint at foot of p. ⌊239⌋
⌊240⌋ blank

Binding:

Boards covered with green silk; medallion in gold with acanthus
leaf motif in centre of front cover; highly decorated spine in gold:
ornament THE ornament/ WORKS OF/ WALTER/ PATER/ ⁚ VOL . I . /
THE RE-/ NAISSANCE/ ornaments/ six in. high decoration with
acanthus leaf design corresponding to that of the medallion on the
front cover/ MACMILLAN & CO.

125

Number published and price:

    775 copies
    Published price 84/- the set; sold in sets only.

Date published:

    Printing ordered 7 June 1900
    Volumes published from September awards

Volume	Title on title-page	
II	MARIUS THE EPICUREAN [in red]/ His Sensations and Ideas. Vol. I iv + 248 pp.	1900
III	MARIUS THE EPICUREAN [in red]/ His Sensations and Ideas. Vol. II. iv + 224	1900
IV	IMAGINARY PORTRAITS [in red]/ and/ GASTON DE LATOUR [in red] / An Unfinished Romance iv + 322 pp.	1900
V	APPRECIATIONS [in red]/ With an Essay on Style iv + 264	1901
VI	PLATO AND PLATONISM [in red]/ A Series of Lectures iv + 284 pp.	1901
VII	GREEK STUDIES [in red]/ A Series of Essays with portrait and tissue guard. iv = 200	1901
VIII	MISCELLANEOUS STUDIES [in red]/ A Series of Essays. iv + 256	1901

    ESSAYS [in red]/ from 'THE GUARDIAN' [in red]
    was published on 4th September 1901 in exactly
    the same format, price 8s. 6d. and can be
    taken as Volume IX of the set.
    THE/ WORKS OF/ WALTER/ PATER is printed on
    the spine as with the other volumes but not
    on the half-title. (U.S.A. $3.00. Sept. 21)

    The above edition does not contain all Pater's writings, nor does
the New Library Edition of 1910.   A list is given at the end of the
later edition of those known items which have not been collected.

An American edition, Edition de Luxe in 8 vols., was published
in 1900-1901 at $3.00 each volume.

Vol. 1. Oct. 1900	Vol. 5. Feb. 1901
2. Dec. 1900	6. Mar. 1901
3. Dec. 1900	7. Mar. 1901
4. Jan. 1901.	8. June 1901

Title-page:

title ⌊in red and black as with the Edition de Luxe⌋/ by WALTER
PATER/ MACMILLAN AND CO. LIMITED/ ST. MARTIN'S STREET, LONDON/ 1910

Imprint:

on blank at end: Printed by R. & R. Clark, Limited, Edinburgh

Format:

Demy octavo   8 7/8" x 5½"

Binding:

Dark-blue cloth; Dust jackets printed in red identical with spine.
Gold lettering and ornaments on spine: Ornament/ Title/ WALTER/
PATER/ medallion ornament/ MACMILLAN AND CO./ ornament

Number published and price:

1250 copies at 7s. 6d. each.

Date of Publication:

Printing ordered 12 March 1910
Issued in monthly volumes - see below

CONTENTS:

I.   THE RENAISSANCE: Studies in Art and Poetry   (June 1910)
       xv + 239 pp.

II.   MARIUS THE EPICUREAN; His Sensations and Ideas. Vol. I
       vi + 243 pp.   (June 1910)

III.   MARIUS THE EPICUREAN: His Sensations and Ideas   Vol.II
       viii + 226 pp.
       (The above two volumes sold together for 15/- net)

IV.   IMAGINARY PORTRAITS   (July 1910)
       iv + 156 pp.

V.   APPRECIATIONS: With an Essay on Style   (Aug. 1910)
       (full title on spine)
       iv + 264 pp.

VI.   PLATO AND PLATONISM A Series of Lectures (Sept.1910)
       iv + 284 pp.

VII.   GREEK STUDIES: A Series of Essays   (Oct. 1910)
       iv + 302 (Portrait with tissue guard)

VIII. MISCELLANEOUS STUDIES: A Series of Essays (Nov. 1910)
       iv + 278 pp.

CONTENTS:

IX.   GASTON DE LATOUR.   An unfinished Romance   (Dec. 1910)
          x + 164 pp.

X.   ESSAYS FROM"THE GUARDIAN"   (May 1910)
          viii + 152

The contents in each case were identical with those of the Edition
de Luxe set.   IMAGINARY PORTRAITS and GASTON DE LATOUR were however
each given a separate volume and ESSAYS FROM "THE GUARDIAN" included as
the tenth volume of the set.

At the end of each volume is a notice: NEW LIBRARY EDITION OF/ THE
WORKS / OF WALTER PATER with a list of the volumes in the edition.

COLLECTED EDITIONS

LIST OF WRITINGS WHICH ARE NOT INCLUDED IN THE 1900/1 AND 1910 EDITIONS

No complete collected edition of the writings of Walter Pater exists: both the 1900/1 and 1910 editions are defective in this sense.   A list is given below of those known items which have not as yet been collected.   The list does not include any work still in manuscript. The number in the CHRONOLOGICAL RECORD in Section I a is given for reference.

PROSE

Title	Year	Section Ia
"Renaissance in Italy: The Age of Despots	1875	No. 19
M. Lemaitres's"Serenus and other Tales"	1877	50
The Life and Letters of Flaubert	1888	59
Wordsworth [Athenaeum: Review]	1889	61
A Poet with Something to Say	1889	63
"It is Thyself"	1889	65
"Toussaint Galabru"	1889	66
"Correspondance de Gustave Flaubert"	1889	68
"A Century of Revolution"	1889	72
A Novel by Mr. Oscar Wilde	1891	79
Introduction to the Purgatory of Dante Alighieri	1892	85
Mr. George Moore as an Art Critic	1893	88

NOTE: The above twelve items were published by Thomas Bird Mosher, Portland, Maine, USA, in UNCOLLECTED ESSAYS BY WALTER PATER (1903)

"Children in Italian and English Design"	1872	11
Imaginary Portraits. 2. An English Poet	1878	29
"Love in Idleness"	1883	33
"The English School of Painting"	1883	35
English at the Universities	1886	44
Vernon Lee's "Juvenalia"	1887	48
Mr. F.W. Bussell	1894	93

NOTE: The above seven papers have not been printed in book form

There are also a number of articles which have not been printed in the two Collected Works in their complete form:

1. Wordsworth

The original essay "On Wordsworth" which appeared in the Fortnightly Review (1874) is different to a great extent from the version which is printed in APPRECIATIONS (1889). Two later Wordsworth reviews were adapted from this paper for later periodical printings (see Appendix b 3: "Wordsworth" for a note on the various versions of the original essay)

2. Coleridge

Only part of the original essay on "Coleridge's Writings" which appeared in the Westminster Review (1866) was used by Pater for the essay "Coleridge" printed in APPRECIATIONS (1889). Most of the missing portion was printed by Albert Mordell in his SKETCHES AND REVIEWS (1919) as "Coleridge as a Theologian" (Mordell's own title). (see Appendix b 4 "Coleridge").

3. "Poems by William Morris"

The last three pages of this review (Westminster Review: 1868) were printed as "Conclusion" in THE RENAISSANCE (1873) and, with revisions, in the 3rd and 4th editions of that book. The revisions are of interest but no note of them appears in any edition of The RENAISSANCE or the collected works.

The earlier portions of the essay were printed in the first edition of APPRECIATIONS (1889) but omitted from the second and later editions and from the collected works. This article was entitled "Aesthetic Poetry" and was printed by Albert Mordell in his SKETCHES AND REVIEWS (1919).

POETRY

Pater wrote a number of poems in his younger days, but did not wish to see them published. Two of these poems (one is 'doubtful') were privately printed by E.H. Blakeney on his private press at Winchester and have not been further published. Blakeney published them in small limited editions which naturally are very scarce and rarely seen. They are:

THE CHANT OF THE CELESTIAL SAILORS (1856)

INSCRIPTION FOR THE LIFE OF WALTER PATER (1859)

They are described in this section, Numbers 13 and 14.

For prose and poetry in manuscript and not yet published, see Section II Unpublished Writings: 'b' 'Manuscripts' and 'c' Poetry.

17.   SELECTIONS FROM WALTER PATER   1901

    Edited, with an Introduction and Bibliography, and notes, by Edward
Everett Hall, Jr. (New York: H. Holt & Co. : 1901) 12mo. lxxvi +
266 pages.   75c. net

18.   THE PATER CALENDAR   1913

    A Quotation from the works of Walter Horatio Pater for every day of
the year, selected by J.M. Kennedy.   (London: Frank Palmer: 1913).
Frontis. Portrait.   Paper back in stiff covers.   There is no contents
or index to give the source of the quotations.

    One would think Pater to be the last author who would be selected
for this form of book, but it makes very good reading.   The 'quotations'
are of good length and well selected.   Kennedy wrote a book: ENGLISH
LITERATURE 1880-1905 [1912] in which he took a gloomy view of the
period: "artistic impotence and artistic philistinism exercise even
separately a melancholy effect" and in an essay on Pater thought "For
Pater's own writing in the end is nothing but another form of euphism".

19.   SELECTIONS FROM WALTER PATER   1924

    Edited, with an introduction, by Ada L.F. Snell (Riverside College
Classics: Boston & New York: Houghton Mifflin: 1924).   12mo. xviii
+ 142 pages.

20.   SELECTED ESSAYS OF WALTER HORATIO PATER   1927

    Edited with an introduction and notes by H.G. Rawlinson M.A.
(Macmillan and Co. Limited: St. Martin's Street, London: 1927).   xviii
+ 183 pages.

    Contents:

        Introduction: Walter Pater

        Style

        Wordsworth

        Charles Lamb

        Shakespeare's English Kings

        Leonardo da Vinci

        The Child in the House

        Romanticism

        Conclusion

Notes

(NOTE: The Introduction contains little of note, being a formal
commentary on each selection.   The notes at the end of the book are of
interest.   There is a short introduction to each essay, then notes on
people or books mentioned by Pater and on classical words and
quotations)

---

21.   WALTER PATER: SELECTED WORKS   1948

Edited by Richard Aldington with an Introduction.   (William
Heinemann Ltd: 1948).   Demy octavo.   557 pages.

Contents:

Introduction

Introductory:
    The Child in the House
    Preface to The Renaissance

England;
    Wordsworth
    Charles Lamb
    Aesthetic Poetry
    Conclusion to The Renaissance
    Dante Gabriel Rossetti

Germany:
    Winckelmann
    Duke Carl of Rosenmold

Low Countries:
    Sebastian van Storck

France:
    Two Early French Stories
    Denys L'Auxerrois
    Suspended Judgment
    A Prince of Court Painters

Italy:
    Pico della Mirandola
    Sandro Botticelli
    Luca della Robbia
    Leonardo da Vinci
    The School of Giorgione

Rome:
    Marius the Epicurean.   2 vols.   1885

Greece:
    The Bacchanals of Euripides
    Lacedaemon

Conclusion:
    Postcript to Appreciations

The book has a dust jacket on which is a sketch of Walter Pater (taken from the Rothenstein etching).

A front page review of this book appeared in the *Times Literary Supplement*, No. 2463 (16 April 1949) 249 as "Pater Preaches".

This is certainly the best volume in this section: the selections are beyond any reasonable reproach; they are of quantity and variety to afford an adequate view of the genius of Walter Pater; and the Introduction, 30 pages, is written by a man who respected his subject and was himself a writer of light and style.

A few days before his death, Richard Aldington wrote to me: "Thank you for what you say about my Introduction to the Selected Pater. I fear it didn't really help much to revive interest in his writings, but I did my best ! "

---

22.   SELECTED WRITINGS: WALTER PATER   1949

Edited and introduced by Derek Patmore (London: The Falcon Press: 1949). Falcon Classics Series, general editor Leonard Russell. 96 pp. cr. octavo.

Contents:

The Renaissance:
Conclusion
Leonardo da Vinci
Sandro Botticelli
The School of Giorgione
Winckelmann

Marius the Epicurean
The Tree of Knowledge
On the Way
Beate Urbs
Two Cirous Houses. I Guests.

Imaginary Portraits
A Prince of Court Painters
Denys l'Auxerrois

Gaston de Latour
Modernity

Appreciations
Dante Gabriel Rossetti

Greek Studies
A Study of Dionysus
Beginnings of Greek Sculpture

Plato and Platonism
The Genius of Plato

NOTE: The 8 pages of Introduction has little of novelty.

It should be pointed out that in no case is a complete item
given.

c. LOCATIONS OF PUBLISHED MANUSCRIPTS

These have all been noted in either Sections I a: CHRONOLOGICAL LIST or Section I b: BOOKS, but for convenience of reference are listed below together with descriptions of the manuscripts if available. The number in Section I a is given.

Number in I a	Title	Location of Manuscript
3	DIAPHANEITÈ	King's School, Canterbury

The manuscript came to the School in the collection of Sir Hugh Walpole, an old boy of the school, who bequeathed his collection to King's. He bound the manuscript and inserted a cutting from a sale catalogue.

The Manuscript is bound in book form, and is of ten leaves.

Pater initialled it "W.H.P. July 1864". It has an O.U.P. rubber stamp on it: "Received at the Oxford Press, Oxford, 21 May 95" and is so stamped on the outside of the first and the last leaf.

Pater's title reads "DIAPHANEITÈ i.e. with a grave accent.

| 18 | A Fragment on MEASURE FOR MEASURE | |
| | | Folger Library, Washington 3, D.C. U.S.A. |

The manuscript comprises 19 sheets.

| 20 | THE MYTH OF DEMETER AND PERSEPHONE | |
| | | Library of Mr. John Sparrow, Warden of All Souls College Oxford |

The manuscript has a fold "no doubt due to enable Pater to carry it in his breast pocket on his journey from Oxford to Birmingham".

It has no title or heading.

Paper: Quarto, blue tinted, slightly deckle-edged.

Number of Pages: 1 - 27 (19 leaves). Only half of p. 25 covered and v. 25 blank and not numbered
Writing: written both sides in smallish writing in black ink.
Alterations: Few, some pages none at all.

Comparison with book:
Some variations were necessary because of the ms. being written for a lecture. For instance: "My object this evening" became "the present essay is an attempt"
There is a little amplification. "Says the Interpreter of the holy places" becomes "Says the prize-poet, or the Interpreter, the Sacristan of the holy places (p. 8i book)

The various translations are unaltered.

Odd words are altered: "ethical stage" becomes "ethical phase."

The main difference however is that some eight passages, not given in the lecture, are inserted in GREEK STUDIES. They are listed below, with the pages of the book for reference:

p. 92 "Homer, in the Iliad, knows Demeter . . . Awake, and sing, ye that dwell in the dust ! " (p. 95)

p. 101 "The worship of Demeter belongs . . . then so fresh and peaceful." (p. 103)

p. 106 "The episode of Triptolemus to whom Demeter . . . at Hermione or Eleusis." (p. 109)

p. 118 "But in the story of Demeter and Persephone . . . the idyll of Theocritus on the Shepherds' Journey."

p. 129 "Some of the modifications of the story of Demeter . . . when the moon looks full upon them." (p. 132)

p. 142 "It is probable that, at a later stage . . . the features of Persephone." (p. 143)

31	THE MARBLES OF AEGINA	The Houghton Library Harvard University Cambridge, Massachusetts

This manuscripts is listed as follows:..

The marbles of Aegina.
A.MS. (unsigned); ⌊n.p., n.d.⌋ 16s. (16p.)
Lecture, which preceded the longer published essay of this title.

32	SAMUEL TAYLOR COLERIDGE	Harvard University U.S.A.
34	DANTE GABRIEL ROSSETTI	Library of a private collector, U.S.A.

Number in I a	Title	Location of Manuscript
42	SIR THOMAS BROWNE	Library of a private collector, U.S.A.
53 - 57 70	GASTON DE LATOUR (Chapters I - V and VII)	The Berg Collection New York Public Library New York

A short description of these manuscripts will be
found in Section I b : GASTON DE LATOUR.
(The unpublished manuscripts of Chapters 8 - 13 of
GASTON survive and are described in Section II:
Unpublished Writings - b. 'Manuscripts')

95	IMAGINARY PORTRAIT	Worcester College Library Worcester College Oxford

This is not a holograph manuscript, but a printing
of the original essay as it appeared in Macmillan's
Magazine (1878) with some slight alterations by
Pater before it was printed by the Daniel Press.
See Section I b: AN IMAGINARY PORTRAIT

96	PASCAL	Bodleian Library Oxford

This fascinating manuscript is in three parts. First
there is the last draft of the essay, taking up 51 pages.
The pages are of quarto size white paper.;the writing
being on alternate lines. The writing is clear and firm
and, for the most part, presents little difficulty to the
reader. Most of the pages are in an advanced state; a
few are heavily scored and amended. There are also a
number of small rectangles of white and blusih paper which
have been placed at the end of the written pages. The
whole has been bound in a neat volume.

The essay was written on the verso of an earlier version
of the essay, which has been crossed out, the two versions
often being opposite to each other. Thus one can study
two states of the piece, or most of the piece, and this
lends interest to the manuscript.

Finally, the earlier pages contain notes for what seems
to be a lecture on Plato's Republic (on which Pater often
lectured at the combined University lectures). (see
Section II b. "Manuscripts" for a short note on these
pages).

SECTION II

UNPUBLISHED WRITINGS

SECTION II   UNPUBLISHED WRITINGS

                    a.   'Lost' items

104.   Chant of the Celestial Sailors when they first
                put out to Sea

105.   Saint Getrude of Himmelstadt

106.   To N.R.N.

107.   Song of the Mermaid

108.   My Cousin

109.   Justification

110.   The Age of Sappho

111.   Dr. Johnson

112.   The School of Phidias

     For information on Nos. 104 to 110 inclusive we are indebted to
Thomas Wright, the biographer of Pater, and in the following notes
references are made to his work: The Life of Walter Pater, 2 vols.
(Everett & Co. 1907)

     Wright undertook to write his life of Pater despite the disapproval
of Pater's two sisters, Hester and Clara.   Once he had started on his
task he went to a great deal of trouble to find all the information he
could regarding Pater's early life and made enquiries by letter or in
person to any surviving friends, acquaintances and relations he could
find.   Without his researches we should know very little of the personal
details of Pater's early life.

     Wright obtained a mass of information from John Rainier McQueen, who
lived at Chailey Hall, Sussex.   McQueen was Pater's closest friend at
King's School, Canterbury, and was blessed with a good memory.   He wrote
a number of letters to Wright, which are now in the Library of Indiana
University.   Wright also stayed with McQueen on two occasions and took
copious notes of their conversations.   It was from McQueen that Wright
obtained information regarding these 'lost' items, and also copies of
Pater's poems (see 'c' of this section).

104 Chant of the Celestial Sailors when they first   Autumn 1858
       put out to Sea

     [Poem]

See Wright, I, 137-138

No quotation is given from this poem

It was written two years after the extant poem: "The Song of the
Celestial Sailors", for which see 'c' in this section.

Wright says that the poem was written during a time of mental
anguish when Pater was assailed by religious doubt and was in a
state of considerable confusion.

105 S. Gertrude of Himmelstadt   Christmas 1858

     [Story in Prose]

See Wright, I, 163-164

This story is said to have contained a song.

Pater is said to have written this during a Christmas spent at
Heidelburg with his Aunt Bessie and his two sisters.

In a letter to Thomas Wright, dated May 22, 1906, McQueen states:
". . . and later, soon after he left school, there was Gertrude of
Himmelstadt, which I read early in 1859".

McQueen gave his opinion, in another latter, dated Nov. 6, 1903
that: "For my part, I prefer the lost "St. Gertrude of
Himmelstadt" to any other prose of Pater's".

An Oxford friend of Pater, Rev. M.B. Moorhouse, borrowed a copy of
this story and turned it into verse.   This version he printed as
"The Rescue: a tale of romantic courage" in Studies in Verse: By
Land and Sea (J.A. Jennings: 1898).   In the Preface, Moorhouse
writes:
     "The first poem has a very pathetic interest to myself, as
     "it was suggested by a tale which my intimate College friend
     "the late Walter Pater told me in the days when we were at
     "Oxford together".

Thomas Wright reprinted Moorhouse's metrical version in his Life
Vol. II, 235-240.   He reports: "McQueen, who was enraptured by
it, said to Mr. Moorhouse, in respect to that young man's metrical
version . . . 'It seems to me you have spoilt it, and distorted
the points of the narrative' "

Moorhouse then tried to borrow the story again, but Pater said he
had burnt it.   "I never grieved more" observed Mr. Moorhouse.
"It was the loveliest story I ever read".

106   To N.R.N.   3 March 1859
      [Poem]

The poem was dated 3rd March 1859, but was lost. See Wright
Vol. I, 161

The following extract is taken from a letter from J.R. McQueen to
Thomas Wright, dated 18 Nov. 1903:

> "when the first, transient, separation took place, Pater
> "wrote a poem 'to N.R.N.' (the final initials of my name
> "JohN RainieR McQueeN) which he had intended to send to
> "me on my approaching birthday, March 3, 1860, as an
> "effort towards reconciliation. I have, I fear, lost
> "this poem, which would have been, now, especially
> "interesting. But I have not seen it for many years".

In a later letter McQueen states that the year was 1859, not 1860

107   Song of the Mermaid   1859
      [Poem]

See Wright, Vol. I, p. 164, whp gives this poem as lost and quotes
the only surviving four lines:

> "The cescent moon falls in the west,
> "Like a mermaid that has lost her lover,
>
>   . . . .
>
> "Which merriest play when drowsy men,
> "Sleep as within their graves".

108   My Cousin   1859
      [Poem]

See Wright, Vol. I, pp. 164-165

Wright quotes the only two known lines:

> "My cousin has a sweet, pale face
>   And dove-meek eyes".

Wright says: "It is remembered that one of the verses was
coloured with recollections of Chailey with its "rhododendrons on
the lawn". (McQueen was the squire of Chailey, Sussex).

McQueen, according to Wright, used to contend that the lady with
the dove-meek eyes was 'the mature Miss Ann Pater of Liverpool".

109   Justification   1859

An essay in prose, now lost.

See Wright, Vol. I, p. 161

In a letter, dated May 22nd 1906, from John Rainier McQueen to
Thomas Wright, this essay was titled "Justification".

We have no extract.

110   The Age of Sappho

See Wright, Vol. II, pp. 116, 128, 197

Wright twice mentions Pater's enthusiasm for Sappho's verse. On
p. 116 of his biography he states that Pater intended to write on
Sappho, and that "The Notes prepared for this article are still in
existence".   On p. 128 he states that Pater "composed an article
on The Age of Sappho , which however was never finished".

We have no date for this.   Wright first mentions the notes on p.
116 which deals with the year 1888, but states "upon whom ⌊Sappho⌋
it was his ambition to write, and upon whom he would have written
if he had lived a little longer".

The notes may be those referred to by Wright on p. 197 when he
quotes Pater as saying: "How I should like to bring out a work
consisting of biographies of these Greek and Latin poets" and then
Wright says: "Beyond making a few notes, however, nothing more was
done."

111   Dr. Johnson

An unfinished study, found in Pater's papers after his death.
It was not published.

The location is not known.

This paper is mentioned by Mrs May Ottley in her Introduction to
"An English Poet" The Fortnightly Review, CXXIX n.s. (April 1931),
pp. 433-434.   "There was found among his papers a certain amount
of fragmentary work, including . . . what promised to be a
characteristically penetrating and illuminating study of Dr.
Johnson . . . "

An unfinished study, found in his papers after Pater's death.
It was almost certainly written during the last few months of his
life.   His last printed essay on Greek Sculpture: "The Age of
Athletic Prizemen" appeared in February, 1894 (see No. 89), so it
is presumed that this followed it.

It is mentioned by his literary executor, Charles Lancelot
Shadwell, in the Preface to the posthumous GREEK STUDIES (1895)
(see No. 97): "The papers on Greek Sculpture are all that remain
of a series which, if Mr. Pater had lived, would probably have
grown into a still more important work.   Such a work would have
included one or more essays on Phidias and the Parthenon, of
which only a fragment, though an important fragment, can be found
amonst his papers; and it was to have been prefaced by an
Introduction to Greek Studies, only a page or two of which was
ever written".

This essay was examined by Lucien Cattan - see Essai sur Walter
Pater (Paris: Picart: 1936), pp. 51-52, in which he states:
"D'autre part, grâce a l'obigeance de Mrs Ottley, j'ai pu avoir
communication d'une esquisse impublishable mais assez avancée ,
intitulee "The School of Phidias" et qui, achevée,aurait pris
place à la suite de The Age of the Athletic Prizemen dans Greek
Studies".   (M. Cattan came to England when engaged on his Essai
and enjoyed the friendship of Mrs May Ottley, then Pater's
executor.   He looked through the remaining Pater manuscripts, and
his bibliography and notes are therefore of great interest).

Cattan states that the manuscript has changed hands many times and
its whereabouts are not known.

Harvard University have an unsigned Pater manuscript, not paged,
not dated, 6s. 7 p, headed 'Introduction to Greek Studies'.

The same library have the following manuscript:

    (The Parthenon)
    A.MS. (unsigned); ⌊n.p., n.d.⌋ 13s. (16p.)
    Evidently part of a longer MS., foliated 25-34, with
    some leaves unnumbered.

b.   Manuscripts

1.   Notes on Plato's Republic

2.   Sundry 'fragments' at Harvard University, USA

3.   Chapters   8 - 13 of GASTON DE LATOUR

Attention is also directed to Section I c: "manuscripts of published writings"

---

1. Notes on Plato's Republic

The manuscript of Pater's essay on "Pascal" is now at the Bodleian (Old) Library, Oxford (see Section I a No. 96 - "Pascal"). The essay was written on one side of the paper only as Pater used writing paper on which parts of an earlier draft of the essay had been sketched out. This was only partly so, for on the verso of pages 14-15, 18-21, 25-27, 29-33 there are holograph notes on Plato. The notes on a number of pages make a consectutive running manuscript. They deal mainly with the Republic and contain passages of translation (probably by Pater himself, but this is not certain) of portions of the dialogue. Chapter IX of PLATO AND PLATONISM is "The Republic" but there seems no correspondence between the book and the notes mentioned here. They might be a draft of a lecture which Pater gave some years earlier on Plato when he was listed on the rota for combined lectures at the University.   He lectured repeatedly on Plato's Republic in the 1870s and 1880s.   (see lists in the Oxford University Gazette).

The manuscripts left by Pater were sold on 15th October 1942 through Messrs Sotheby at a special sale in aid of the Red Cross (the various lots in that sale make fascinating reading for collectors). They were sold in two lots:

Lot No. 592

PATER (WALTER) Author's holograph MSS on several hundred 4to sheets, notes of Lectures on Plato; The Marbles of Aegina; Gandioso the Second; and other Essays. 4to.

Lot No. 593

PATER (WALTER) Gaston de Latour, Author's holograph MS of Chapters 8 - 13 on 158 4to sheets
These chapters are believed to be unpublished. An important literary manuscript.

2.   Lot No. 592 is now in the Houghton Library, Harvard University, Cambridge, Massachussets, USA.   This accesssion is listed as follows:

Pater, Walter, 2839-1894,
Literary and scholarly papers:

(i)   — —— .
        Plato's ethics.
        A. MS. (unsigned); ⌊n.p., n.d.⌋ 12s. (21p.)

(2)   —— – .
        ⌊Essay on Plato: fragment⌋
        A.MS. (unsigned);   [n.p., n.d.] 5s.(5p.)
        Numbered 19-23;   perhaps a continuation of "Plato's ethics."

(3)   – — — .
        ⌊The history of philosophy⌋
        A.MS.(unsigned); ⌊n.p., n.d.⌋ 24s. (46p)

(4)   – — — .
        ⌊Gaston de Latour⌋
        A.MS. (unsigned);   ⌊n.p.,n.d.⌋ 13s.(16p.)
        Comprises: a fragment of ch. 8, a fragment of ch. 12, a leaf of notes, and ch.13, the last evidently in the autograph of Clara Pater.

(5)   – — — .
        Tibalt the Albigense.
        A.MS.(unsigned); [n.p., n.d.] 19s.(19p.)

(6)   – — — .
        Introduction to Greek Studies.
        A.MS.(unsigned); ⌊n.p.,n.d.⌋ 6s.(7p.)

(7)   – — — .
        The aesthetic life.
        A.MS.(unsigned); ⌊n.p.,n.d.⌋ 39s.(39p.)

(8)   – — — .
        Gaudioso, the second.
        A.MS.(unsigned); ⌊n.p.,n.d.⌋ 21s.(21p.)

(9)   – — — .
        [Translations from Plato⌋
        A.MS.(unsigned); ⌊n.p.,n.d.⌋ 38s.(69p.)
        Evidently written at several different periods.

(10)   – — — .
        ⌊Translation from unidentified French source or sources⌋
        A.MS.(unsigned); ⌊n.p.,n.d.⌋ 45s(49p.)

(11)   Pater, Walter, 1839-1894.
         Art & Religiom.
         A.MS.(unsigned); [n.p.,n.d.] 74f.(81p.)
         Discontinuous and fragmentary; the title at head
         may be for the work, or only one section.

(12)   - - .
         The writings of Cardinal Newman.
         A.MS.(unsigned); [n.p.,n.d.] 24s.(26p.)

(13)   - - - .
         [English Literature]
         A.MS. (unsigned); [n.p.,n.d.] 34s.(38p.)
         Discontinuous; more than half dealing with Chaucer.

(14)   - - - .
         [The Parthenon]
         A.MS.(unsigned); [n.p.,n.d.] 13s.(16p.)
         Evidently part of a longer MS., foliated 25-34 with
         some leaves unnumbered.

(15)   - - - .
         [Evil in Greek Art]
         A.MS.(unsigned); [n.p.,n.d.] 5s.(10p.)
         A fragment.

(16)   - - - .
         The Marbles of Aegina.
         A.MS. (Unsigned); [n.p.,n.d.] 16s.(16p.)
         Lecture which preceded the longer published essay of
         this title.

(17)   - - - .
         [Moral philosophy]
         A.MS. (unsigned); [n.p.,n.d.] 26s.(51p.)
         Possibly a lecture, though notes show it was
         considered for insertion in Marius.

(18)   - - - .
         [Hobbes]
         A.MS.(unsigned); [n.p.,n.d.] 14s.(14p.)

(19)   - - - .
         [Dante]
         A.MS.(unsigned), [n.p.,n.d.] 8s.(8p.)

(20)   - - - .
         [Notre Dame de Troyes]
         A.MS.(unsigned); [n.p.,n.d.] 7s.(7p)

(21)   - - - .
         [The young romantic]
         A.MS.(unsigned); [n.p.,n.d.] 5s.(10p.)
         Incomplete at either end.

(22)   Pater, Walter 1839-1894
         [Miscellaneous notes and fragments]
         A.MS.(Unsigned); [v.p.,n.d.] 75s.(95p.)
         Some of these may be associated with identified MSS.
         elsewhere in the collection.

(23)   - - - .
         [Miscellaneous brief notes]
         A.MS.(unsigned); [n.p.,n.d.] 1 folder.

(24)   Symonds, John Addington, 1840-1893, ascribed author.
         Arezzo
         MS. (unidentified hand); [n.p.,n.d.] 16s.(16p.)
         First entitled "Prelude to Michelangelo." Annotated
         by Walter Pater. Ascribed by an unidentified hand to
         Symonds, but not located in Symonds's works, and not in
         his autograph.

NOTE: The above Accessions Record is reproduced by kind
        permission of the Curator of Manuscripts, The Houghton
        Library, Harvard University, USA.

3.   Chapters 8 - 13 of GASTON DE LATOUR

      Lot No. 593 (see above) is in the library of Mr. John Sparrow,
All Souls College, Oxford.   In Section I b BOOKS: No. 9 - Gaston de
Latour this lot is described together with other manuscripts of GASTON

c. Poetry

NOTE: To complete the survey of surviving poetry written by Pater,
        one should take account of the poem: "The Chant of the
        Celestial Sailors" printed and published by Edward Henry
        Blakeney on his private press at Winchester in 1928 (see
        section I a No. 1 and section I b No. 13).   There is a further
        poem: "Inscription for Ye Life of Walter PaterQ which will be
        found in Wright's The Life of Walter Pater, Vol. I, p. ⌊vi⌋
        which may be by Pater (see section I a No. 2 and I b No. 14).

NOTE ON THE POEMS

For information on the poetry written by Pater, and for copies of
those poems which have survived, we are largely indebted to Thomas
Wright. When preparing his biography The Life of Walter Pater, 2 vols
Everett & Co. 1907), he sought out as many of Pater's early friends as
possible. Two of them, John Rainier McQueen of Chailey, Sussex, and
the Rev. M.N. Moorhouse, of Bath, gave what information they could, and
were each able to supply him with copies of some of the poems.

In the notes to each poem I refer to hisbiography. Statements
made by McQueen, unless otherwise attributed, are quoted from the
letters which he wrote to Thomas Wright, letters which are now in the
possession of Indiana University, and to whom I am indebted for copies
of the complete correspondence.

McQueen wrote to Wright, 6 November 1903: "Pater . . . composed
many poems while he was at school" [King's School, Canterbury].   In
another letter, 22 May 1906: "Pater's literary activity really began
very early — certainly before he was 17 or even 16. His poems were
numerous — enough to fill a large part of a MS book, not very thin."

I now quote from WrightVol. I, 98-99: " . . . for not only was
Pater one of the most prolific schoolboy authors who ever lived; but
as an undergraduate, he wrote something or other — a poem, a
translation, a portion of an essay — almost every day, while at King's
School he composed, in addition to the "streaming themes" laid before
the good Mr. Fisher, scores of poems . . . It was his custom to enter
the poems in a manuscript book kept for the purpose, and then to make
copies for those of his friends who begged them. The best seem to
have appeared in print — having possibily been contributed to the
Poet's Corner of some country newspaper." In a footnote to this,
Wright states "Pater told his friends that some of his early writings
had been printed. The school magazine of King's was not functioning in
Paters time, and extensive search in local and county newspapers has
not brought to life anything by Pater.

Now for Wright, Vol. I, 199: "Having cast aside Christianity, Pater
now tried to obliterate all his connections with it. First he burnt
his manuscript volume of poems — not because he thought lightly of their
merits, but simply because of their Christian tone, though it should
not be overlooked that he had recently been reading Goethe's Wahrheit
und Dichtung with its account of a similar holocaust. . . . He did
not forget that he had lent the book to McQueen and Moorhouse with full
permission to copy out what poems they pleased and to do what they liked
with them; nor did he ever request the destruction of their copies.
His only desire, indeed, was to remove the sight of them from his own
eyes."

I have Thomas Wright's copies of the poems listed at the head of
this section, made from originals shewn to him by McQueen and the Rev.

Moorhouse.   In addition I have copies of MSS. made by McQueen himself,
and other copies which I think were made by Moorhouse.   All these are
in a small some-made file belonging to homas Wright;

                    Poems of Walter Pater

with a label on which Wright wrote:

                    Most of these were copied from the originals by

                    me - Thomas Wright - when visiting Mr McQueen,

                    Pater's friend at Chailey Sussex 26 April 1904.

                    Others are from copies sent to me by Mr.

                    McQueen.

    McQueen assured T. Wright that he had the originals of many more
poems written by ater, but despite much solicitation by Wright, he
could nor produce them.

    We now come to the question of the authenticity of these poems.
I homas Wright was a gullible man: an upright man, yet inclined to
accept everything told to him as true, and had very little critical
powers.   However, he certainly saw poems in holograph manuscript
which seemed to be by Pater, and in some instances bore his signature.
Rainier was a truly eccentric person, extremely opinionated and
quarrelsome (he once ordered a carriage to drive up to his front door,
then commended his wife to get in it and l ave him and her home at once)
This does not infer however that he was untruthful.   There is the
additional evidence of Wright's meeting and correspondence with the Rev.
Moorhouse, who also had copies of some of Pater's poems.   Moorhouse had
some literary pretensions, and was well thought of in his Bath parish.

    The poems have a homogeneous quality and there is little doubt that
they were composed by the same person.   Certain elements are common to
the poems: a religious fervour combined with an impassioned love of
nature, though nature seems to have filled the writer with awe and
foreboding rather than joy and certainty.   This sense of foreboding
inclined him to hark back to some golden age when the stresses of
modern life did not apply.   At times there is present a longing for
rest, almost stoical, and at times resembling Arnold.

    Only one poem certainly by Pater has yet been published: THE CHANT
OF THE CELESTIAL SAILORS (Section I a No. 1; I b No. 13) and this was
in a privately printed edition of 30 copies only, thus few people will
have seen this specimen of the poetry Pater wrote in his early days.
I am therefore printing one further illustrative poem: "Sonnet: Oxford
Life" dated 27 March 1860

113.   "The Legend of Saint Elizabeth of Hungary"   1856

See __Wright__Vol. I, 98 99 - 101

I have two copies of this poem, one in the hand of John Rainier
McQueen, the other written out by T. Wright.   Neither contains a date,
but the McQueen copy states, at the end of the poem: "I believe Pater
gave me this copy of his ballad of S. Elizabeth of Hungary early in
1856, but I understood it had been written some little time before.
J.R.M."

In the bibliography appended to his biography, Vol. II, 254, Wright
places the poem as first item, and dates it "1856 Spring" but this may
be a conjecture on his part.

The poem seems to be unsigned.

This poem is of seven stanzas, each stanza containing three rhymed
couplets.   Each line has seven iambic feet, the fourteener, a most
unusual prosodic line.

The poem tells the story of S. Elizabeth and of a miracle
associated with her.   T. Wright states that the poem was "avowedly
suggested by the perusal of Kingsley's dramatic poem, __The Saint's__
__Tragedy, or the True Story of Saint Elizabeth of Hungary__, which
appeared in 1848."

114.   "Poets Old and New"   August 1856

See __Wright__   Vol. I. 98 and 102. He quotesthe last verse of the
poem.

There are two separate copies of the poem; one written by Thomas
Wright, the other I think by Rev. Moorhouse. Both are dated:
"Canterbury August 1856".   The Moorhouse copy has a signature (copy)
"W.H. Pater"

There are eleven four line stanzas, with alternate rhyming.   The
poem is written in iambic feet, the four lines of each stanza taking
5, 3, 5, 2 feet.

The poet looks with longing at the idyllic life of poets in former
ages and contrasts this with the "din of ceaseless labour" in modern
towns.

115.   "Cassandra"   June 29th 1857

See Wright Vol. I, 118-119.

There are two copies of this poem. One written out by Thomas Wright
the other by John Rainier McQueen. Both subscribed: "Signed, W.H.
Pater. June 29: 1857."   The McQueen copy has at the head of the
manuscript: "Poems written by W.H. Pater, while a King's Scholar at
Canterbury". It is numbered ' 3 '

The poem, the longest in the file, has 15 stanzas, each of 8 lines,
with alternate lines in uncertain rhyme, and a pervading imabic
measure.

McQueen wrote to Thomas Wright, 16 Nov. 1903:

            "I enclose W.H. Pater's 'Cassandra'. I like it less
            "than most of Pater's verse, and I think you will see
            "in it a decided declension from the high moral and
            "religious, I might say spiritual, tone of the 2
            "earlier poems which I sent you last week."

The two earlier poems mentioned were "The Legend of S. Elizabeth of
Hungary" and "The Chant of the Celestial Sailors".   T. Wright wrote
of the poem as "mournful and slightly sensual".

In a note to stanza 14 of the copy made by McQueen, he states:
This stanza and the 2 that follow are in a different, and I think a
female hand.   Probably W.H.P. got one of his sisters to help him in
copying out for me this long, and I must say, tedious and dreary
ballad. J.R.M."

In the poem Cassandra laments her unhappy lot "crouching in a
tyrant thrall" and appeals to Apollo to close her eyes in "endless
darkness".

116.   "Watchman, what of the Night ? "   Summer 1858

See Wright I. 136 and 137

The copy was written by Thomas Wright. It is headed by a
quotation: "The Watchman said The morning cometh and also the night, if
ye will enquire, enquire ye.   IS. XXI II, 12 "

It is dated "Summer 1858.

The copy contains ten stanzas, each of nine lines, with alternate
lines in rhyme, each line taking five iambic feet.

The poem is a sombre reflection on the loneliness and gloom of the
night scene.

117.   "The Acorn"   October 1859

    See <u>Wright</u> Vol. I 180 and 181

    The copy is in the hand of Thomas Wright.

    It is headed:

                    The Acorn

                Written in a German Album

                Heidelberg Oct. 1859

and (copy) signed W.H. Pater

    The poem consists of seven stanzas , each of 4 lines, with rhyme
scheme a b b a, each line having four iambic feet.

    The growth of the acorn inspired hope that the owner of the album
would grow as a goodly tree "In God's wide garden of the world".

118.   "Sonnet: Oxford Life"   27 March 1860

    See <u>Wright</u> Vol. I 192 and 193-194

    There are two copies of this sonnet, in identical text; one made
by Thomas Wright, the other I judge by Rev. M.B. Moorhouse.

    As mentioned in NOTE ON THE POEMS above I am printing this short
poem as an illustration of Pater's early poetry.   See overleaf:

OXFORD LIFE

Brown hedge rows - furrowed fields - with here and there
   A brighter patch of greenness - dimly seen,
   Glints forth a silver streamlet, caught between
Low thickets of grey willows, clipt and bare,
Vexed by the chill March wind: but far away
   Along the South, rise up the Berkshire hills,
   Not sleeping but intent, as one who wills
Strongly, - athwart their slopes one sunny ray:
   And that bold outline to the scene imparts
   A spirit and a word for wakeful hearts,
And my poor life, - I feel the starting tears ! -
   That should be conscious spirit, Earth reproves
   Which cannot read the law by which it moves.
Oh ! for a godlike aim thro' all these silent years !

March 27, 1860

119.　"The Fan of Fire:　A Study from Wordsworth"　　1860

See **Wright**　Vol. I　180　and　182-183

This copy, in the Handwriting of Thomas Wright, is dated 29 March 1860.

The poem consists of eight stanzas of 8 lines each, with a rhyming scheme in which lines 2 and 4, 6 and 8 are in rhyme.　The measure is iambic, alternately of four and three feet.　There is a final stanza of twelve lines with lines 2 and 4, 6 and 8, 1o and 12 in rhyme.

The Fan of Fire is the poet's impression of the sunrise as seen from the banks of the river Rhine.　It is a hymn to nature which however fills him with dread of the future.

120.　"Greek Minstrel's Song from 'Iphigenia' "

See **Wright**　Vol. I　192 and 194

There are two copies of this poem, one made by Thomas Wright, the other I judge by Rev. M.B. Moorhouse.

This poem consists of five stanzas, each of three lines, all three lines have identical rhyme.　The line is of five iambic feet,

In 5 May 1904, McQueen wrote to Thomas Wright:　"Thanks for copying out Pater's poem Iphigenia for me . . . it illustrates the state of his mind when we parted in 1860"

As with the previous poem, "The Fan of Fire", the wonders of nature fill the poet with unease.

APPENDICES

APPENDICES

a. THOMAS BIRD MOSHER: MAN OF LETTERS

Thomas Bird Mosher was born in Bideford, Maine, near the sea, September 11th 1853, the son of Benjamin and Mary Elizabeth (Merrill) Mosher. His father was a sailor by profession and was the captain of a sailing ship at the date when his son was born. He received some education at public schools in Bideford, and then at Boston, to which town his family moved, but he always claimed that it was his father who gave him his greatest education when he allowed him to go to sea for long voyages, once for five years. These voyages fostered his love for reading and he early developed that remarkable flair for the rare and choice in books which later made his library one of the most famous private collections in America.

His career in the book world began when he was employed as a clerk-bookkeeper in the publishing house of Dresser and McLellan in Exchange Street, Portland, Maine, in 1871, and practically all his business life was passed in Portland. From 1881 to 1890 he was one of the partners of the firm known as McLellan, Mosher and Co. He came into touch with the particular interest which proved to be the ruling passion of his life: the desire to publish books according to his ideas on how they should be published. His firm unfortunately became insolvent, but nothing daunted he somehow managed to borrow sufficient money to start a small publishing business of his own.

Mosher's first published book was Modern Love and Other Poems by George Meredith which he brought out in (Oct.) 1891. It faithfully reproduced the text of the 1862 edition, and was later revised and issued with other poems by Meredith in Mosher's 'Old World Series'. He published some 500 titles, using beautiful papers, sometimes specially imported for him, and printing with the finest fonts available to him to produce lovely small books in bindings of the highest taste.

Although famous among all men of literary insight and sympathy in every nation and country where rare and beautiful books are read and cherished, he was entirely inknown to a great majority of the people of Portland. He lived a life withdrawn from most of the ordinary modern activities; and except for a small circle of warm and faithful friends his figure was not seen among any of the social groups of Portland. He had a little shop consisting of a few simple rooms up a dusty flight of stairs at No.45 Exchange Street, which contained little of the elaborate machinery of modern business. There he was fortunate in the faithful and highly efficient service of his secretary, Miss Flora Lamb, a typist or two, and a man to fill the mail orders.

Among the most noted of Mosher's reprints were the American edition of 'The Germ' in 1898; Swinburne's Poems and Ballads in 1899; Rossetti's poetical works in 1902; and the first facsimile reprint of Fitzgerald's translation of Omar Khyyam. In addition to these he edited and compiled a bibliography in his 'Old World Series' of FitzGerald's entire text of Omar. In 1894 he began publishing and editing The Bibelot, a monthly magazine of reprints of works he thought worthy of reproduction. This periodical was continued to 1914. Mosher's final volume was a beautiful edition of The Odes, Sonnets and Lyrics of John Keats.

In 1901 he paid a visit to England where he was well received and where he met so many of the people with whom he had corresponded.

He was a member of clubs and societies in USA and other countries, among these were the Bibliographical Society of London and the Grolier Club of New York. In 1901 he was granted an honorary degree of Master of Arts by Bowdain College.

In July 1892 he married Anne M. Littlefield of Saco. He died of asperio-sclerosis at his lovely home 30 Highfield Street, Portland, on 30th August 1923. He left two sons, Harrison Hume Mosher and Thomas Bird Mosher, Jr. His press continued publication for a time under the direction of his faithful secretary, Miss Lamb, on behalf of Mrs. Mosher

His publications were a marvel of good taste in many ways. He assiduously provided bibliographical details for the reader; wrote appreciative introductions; and often printed, together with the text selected, auxiliary material, such as poems on the subject of the book, and gave the impress of a loving directing mind. The books and periodicals themselves were produced in neat and pleasant format, on good quality paper, and compare well with any other publications of his time. They were offered as parts of various series: English Reprint; Old World; Brocade, and others. Their prices were very reasonable and the sales satisfactory.

This brings us to consider Mosher as a business man. His love for literature and fine books cannot be doubted, but it is interesting to find that this did not mean that he was not an acute publicity minded man and a successful man of business. The remarkable aspect of his career was that over a long period of time he managed to produce what amounted to private press books, of a high standard of content, and sell the books in sufficient quantities to make a satisfactory income for himself.

He was involved from time to time in controversy by reason of his literary 'piracy'. As the International Copyright Convention did not apply to America, he could legally, if not ethically, print English books, or rather the works of English writers, at will. He was frequently assailed for this, but pocket and principle were satisfied, as far as he was concerned, because (a) having to author to pay, he could produce books of quality at popular prices and still make a handsome profit; and (b) he thus introduced good literature to a wide American public which would not otherwise have known it. I quote him: "Confessedly, my work has opened the gates of a luminous world to me. And for this very reason I would transmit what light I may to others, even as in the races of old, relays of runners passed on the burning torch." "Moreover, I see the thing of beauty in art, in letters, in music, - in a word, the beauty of an idea, - is given to few to create, while to enjoy should be the inalienable birthright of all. Conceivably this thing of beauty might be hidden in the obscurity of.

woeful type and wrietched paper, at what risk of almost absolute
effacement. "

One of Mosher's idols was Walter Pater, whose writings he so often
printed, and this is a suitable place to list the papers and books of
Pater which were printed by Mosher.   The list which now follows is
divided into two parts: I. The reprints and extracts in the magazine
The Bibelot, and   II. Books reprinted in various series.

Before giving the lists, I give below a few books and periodicals
which could be consulted by the reader should he or she wish to learn
more about the genial Mosher:

    Chapman, Alfred K.
        "Thomas Bird Mosher".
            Colby Library Quarterly, Feb. 1958, Ser. IV, 229-244

        A full account of Mosher's life and work.   There is a large
        Mosher collection at Colby College.

    Hatch, B.L.
        A check list of the publications of Thomas Bird Mosher of
        Portland, Maine - MDCCCXCI - MDCCCCXXIII - compiled and
        edited by Benton L. Hatch and with a biographical essay by
        Ray Nash - Printed at the Gehenna Press for the University
        of Massachusetts Press.   MCMLXVI.

        The reader should not be misled by the modest title. This
        is a sumptuous book and its content represents the fruits of
        many years of research by an accomplished scholar.

    Huntress, Keith G.
        Thomas Bird Mosher: A Bibliographical and Literary Study
        (Dissertation for the University of Illinois).
            1912. 145 pages.

    Mathews, Fred V.
        Thomas Bird Mosher
            Portland: 1941

    Morley, Christopher.
        John Mistletoe
            1931.   p. 386

    Newton, A.G.
        This Book-Collecting Game
            Boston: Little, Brown & Co. : 1928

        pp. 119-125 deals with Mosher.   Very few facts are given, but
        a sympathetic appreciation made of his work.
        "With the limited means at his disposal he produced books which
        were beautiful in type and format, were easy to read and easy to
        hold; moreover they had this merit: they were published at a
        price which put them within the reach of all.

Pottle, F.A.
"Aldi Discipulus Americanus" in Mosher's Amphora, Vol. 2.
First published in Literary Review, Dec. 29th 1923, N.Y.

Tinker, E.L.
"New Editions, Fine and Otherwise",
New York Times Book Review 5 October 1941, p. 28

Van Trump , James D. and Ziegler, Arthur P. Jr.
"Thomas Bird Mosher: Publisher and Pirate"
The Book Collector utumn 1962, pp. 295-312.

This article gives a careful if rather one-sided account of
Mosher the Pirate. It makes very interesting reading and
contains several plates of Mosher's publications.

Local journals contained many references to Mosher at the time
of his death, and in later editions:

Portland Evening Express. September 1, 1962
"Thomas Bird Mosher"

Maine Library Bulletin

Portland Public Library literature

The following American libraries hold complete sets of The Bibelot:

New York State Library
Educational Building, Albany 1
New York

New York Public Library
5th Avenue and 42nd Street
New York 18

Portland Public Library
619 Congress Street
Portland, Maine

"It is in Italy, in the fifteenth century . . .   15
    many-sided, centralised, complete"
    [Quotation from the "Preface" to The Renaissance, pp.
    xii - xiii. See Section No. Ia No. 1]
    III, p. [286], September 1897

Two items on Pater:

Benson, A.C.
    Quotation from his biography Walter Pater (1906) p. 63:
    "Perhaps it may be thought that Pater's judgment of Lamb
    . . . though the picture they may draw is incontestably
    truer to detail".
    XII p. [220] July 1906

Johnson, Lionel.
    "Walter Pater"   Poem.
    X. pp. 94 - [96]   March 1904

    This is too long to print here but the poem is full of
    splendid thought expressed in sumptuous language:

    "With cloistral jealousness of ardour strove
        to guard her sacred grove"

----

b.   Books reprinted in varies series

The Child in the House.   An Imaginary Portrait   27
    Brocade Series I. (1895). 46 pp.
    Fourteen editions of this book were published
    down to 1908.

The Child in the House
    Vest Pocket Series. XVII. (1909). xviii + 42 pp.   27

Denys l'Auxerrois. An Imaginary Portrait.   43
    Brocade Series. VIII (1898). 54 pp.
    Second edition, Sept. (1898)

Duke Carl of Rosenmold. An Imaginary Portrait   46
    Brocade Series. X (1898) 60 pp.
    Second edition, Sept. (1898)

Emerald Uthwart. An Imaginary Portrait.   83
    Brocade Series. XV. (1898)   84 pp.
    Second edition, June 1900

Essays from the 'Guardian'.   100
    "Reprints of Privately Printed Books" I.
    1897. 164 pp.   (See also Section Ib No. 10)
    Second edition 1898

Gaston de Latour. An Unfinished Romance   99
    Old World Series XLIII (see also Section Ib. No. 9)
    1906. 132 pp.

Marius the Epicurean. His Sensations and Ideas   36
    The Quarto Series (1900) 8 (See alsoSection ib. No. 2)
    2 vols. I. XXVI + 211; II 209 pp.

A Prince of Court Painters. An Imaginary Portrait   37
    Brocade Series VII (1898) 64 pp.
    Second edition in Sept. 1898.
    Third edition July 1906

The Renaissance   Studies in Art and Poetry   16
    Quarto Series. IX (1902) (See also Section ib.No. 1)
    XX + 248 pp.

The Renaissance   Studies in Art and Poetry   16
    Miscallaneous SeriesLVII. (1912) 304 pp.
    Second edition published in 1924.

Sebastian van Storck. An Imaginary Portrait.   41
    Brocade Series X. (1898). 60 pp. (August)
    Second edition September 1898

UNCOLLECTED ESSAYS   101
    Miscellaneous Series. 1903.
    See Section Ib. No. 11

Some Great Churches in France: Three Essays by William Morris   91)
    and Walter Pater.   94)
    Brocade Series (1903). VII + 108 pp.
    (Pater's essays were Notre Dame d'Amiens and Vezelay)
    Second edition December 1905.
    Third edition November 1912.

The Story of Cupid and Psyche done out of the Latin of   36
    Apuleius.
    Brocade Series (1897). IV. 54 pp. (April)
    Six editions published up to 1909.

NOTE: Fuller details regarding format etc. will generally be found
    on consulting the references to Section Ia or Ib.

APPENDICES

b.   Multi-form articles — a selection

1. "Aesthetic Poetry"

We are here to consider the first two versions of this paper:

PWM.   "Poems by William Morris"
        Westminster Review, XXIV n.s. (October 1868), 300-312
        (See Section Ia: Chronological Record — No. 6)
        The latter part of this review, pp. 309-312, became
        the "Conclusion" of STUDIES IN THE HISTORY OF THE
        RENAISSANCE (1873).

AP   "Aesthetic Poetry"
        APPRECIATIONS (1889) 213 - 227

     The article "Aesthetic Poetry" printed in SKETCHES AND REVIEWS
need not be considered here as it is merely a reprint from the
APPRECIATIONS version.   It was included by the editor, Albert Mordell,
as this essay had been omitted by Pater from the second edition of
APPRECIATIONS and was not to be found in the two collected editions of
Pater's works.

     There is a slight air of mystery about the 1868 Morris review.
From time to time Pater supplied lists of his writings to enquirers,
but never listed the review.   The Bodleian Library hold a holograph
'biography' written by Pater and this item is not given in it. Further
when his friend and literary executor Charles L. Shadwell published the
posthumous MISCELLANEOUS STUDIES in 1895 he provided 'a brief
chronological list of his published writings' in which he includes
"Aesthetic Poetry, Written 1868. First published 1889 in Appreciations"
with no mention of the Morris review.   Ferris Greenslet in his book
Walter Pater (Heinemann: 1900) also appended a "Chronology" and merely
copied Shadwell's entry.

     There are many differences between PWM and AP. Some of them arise
from the fact that, whereas PWM was written as a review of specific
books of poetry, AP was intended as a literary essay on a subject
rather than on any particular books. It was therefore necessary to
adjust various expressions to remove traces of the review structure.
Thus PWM commences, p. 300:

          "This poetry is neither a mere reproduction of Greek or
          mediaeval life . . . "

but this had to be changed in AP, p. 213 to:

          "The aesthetic poetry is neither a mere reproduction of
          Greek or mediaeval poetry . . . "

With the same object in view Pater omitted most of the quotations in

164

PWM for the later version. There are a number of lengthy passages similarly omitted which are concerned with criticism or examination of the poetry in the books originally reviewed.

There are other revisions however which show significant changes of thought, expression and stress in AP when compared to PWM. Some of these are quoted below:

PWM. p. 301: "That religion chades into sensuous love, and sensuous love into religion has often been seen."

AP. p. 215: "That religion, monastic religion at any rate, has its sensuous side, a dangerously sensuous side, has been often seen;"

PWM. p. 301: "a poeple whose loss was in the life of the senses only by possession of an idol, the beautiful idol of the Latin hymn writers, who for one moral or spiritual sentiment have a hundred sensuous images. Only by the inflaming influence of such idols can any religion compete with the presence of the fleshly lover."

AP. P. 215: "a people whose loss was in the life of the senses partly by its aesthetic beauty, a thing so profoundly felt by the Latin hymn-writers, who for one moral or spiritual sentiment have a hundred sensuous images

Again, on p. 302 PWM we have the following passage which Pater thought it wise to omit from AP:

"Who knows whether, when the simple belief in them has faded "away, the most cherished sacred writings may not for the first "time exercise their highest influence as the most deoicate "amorous poetry in the world"

PWM. p. 302 "The idolatry of the cloister" becomes
AP. p. 216 "The devotion of the cloister"

PWM p. 302: "Quite in the way of one who handles the older sorceries the Church has a thousand charms to make the absent near. Like the woman in the idyll of Theocritus . . . it is the cry of all her bizarre rites"

AP. p. 216: "But then, the Church, that new Sibyl, had a thousand secrets to make the absent near"

PWM p. 302: "That the whole religion of the middle age was but a beautiful disease or disorder of the senses."

AP. p. 217: "That the monastic religion of the Middle Age was, in fact, in many of its bearings, like a beautiful disease or disorder of th senses

The difference in the trend of thought shown over more than twenty years is illustrated by the above extracts and the reader is left to muse on the change, if only in discretion between the Pater of 1868 ans the man of 1889.

b.   Multi-form articles

                    2.   "Conclusion"

                          The Renaissance

    The interest of this famous article partly lies in the fact that
Pater published four versions, the first appearing in 1868, the last in
1893. Thus they cover the greater part of his writing life and help to
illustrate changes in both his style and in his creed.

    The four "Conclusions" are:

    PWM.   "Poems of William Morris" [review]
            Westminster Review, XXXI n.s. (October) 1868
            The "Conclusion" was the last four pages,
            309-312 . (The first part of the review was
            published as "Aesthetic Poetry" in the first
            edition of APPRECIATIONS (1889)

    RI.   The essay was now published separately under
            the title "Conclusion" in the first edition of
            STUDIES IN THE HISTORY OF THE RENAISSANCE (1873)
            It was the final paper in that book, taking pp.
            207 - 213.

    R3.   "Conclusion" was omitted from the second edition
            of the book (1877) but published in the third
            edition, renamed THE RENAISSANCE: STUDIES IN
            ART AND POETRY (1888)

    R4.   Fourth edition of The Renaissance (1893)

    A close collation of PWM and RI reveals 36 points of difference.
They fall into two very unequal groups: (1) Alterations of a minor
character which had been made solely to clarify the expression and
improve the style of writing.   They number 34, and can be subdivided
into 23 alterations in punctuation and 11 verbal improvements. (2)
There are the two remaining alterations, which concern the meaning of
the writer and produce a fresh emphasis, or lack of emphasis would be
the more accurate phrase. , Pater prepared everything he wrote with the
greatest care.   In 1963 the oldest known Brasenose graduate told me
that he remembers Pater saying to him: "I never publish anything
until I have written it out seven times."

    Though the alterations in punctuation are not significant it may be
of interest to quote one instance:

    PWM. p. 310: "But when reflection begins to act upon those
            objects they are dissipated under its influence, the
            cohesive force is suspended like a trick of magic,
            each object is loosed into a group of impressions,
            colour, odour, texture, in the mind of the observer."

                            166

R1. p. 208-209: "But when reflection begins to act upon
        objects they are dissipated under its influence; the
        cohesive force is suspended like a trick of magic;
        each object is loosed into a group of impressions, -
        colour, odour, texture, - in the mind of the observer."

The second version is not only easier to understand but has a certain
rhythmical cadence (W.J. Courthope in a review of THE RENAISSANCE
Quarterly Review, CXXXVII (October 1874) thundered: "this is plain,
downright, unmistakable poetry").

Here is an example of a verbal revision.

        PWM. p. 312: "Well, we are all condamnés, as Victor Higo
                somewhere says: we have an interval and then we
                cease too be."

        R1. p. 212: "Well, we are all condamnes, as Victor Hugo says:
                les hommes sont tous condamnés a morte avec des sursis
                indéfinis: we have an interval, and then our place
                knows us no more"

The vague "somewhere" was omitted (it was from Les Miserables); further
by giving the quotation in full the meaning of "condamnés" is made clear
It explains to what we are condemned and under what conditions.

    These extracts illustrate Pater as a craftsman; much more
interesting is the second group of revisions, though only two in number.
The first concerns the omission of one entire paragraph.   Between the
paragraph in the review ending "that strange perpetual weaving and
unwaving of ourselves" and that commencing "Philsophiren, says Novalis,
ist dephlegmatisiren, vivificiren.(PWM. 311; R1 210) the following
paragraph is found:

        "Such thoughts seem desolate at first;   at times all the
        "bitterness of life seems concentrated in them.   They bring the
        "image of one washed out beyond the bar in a sea at ebb, losing
        "even his personality, as the elements of which he is composed
        "pass into new combinations.   Struggling as he must to save
        "himself, it is himself that he loses at every moment."

All the respect which this paragraph may command for its metaphor and
style cannot veil the clear meaning of the message.   This is the logical
conclusion of the doctrine of the flux: "it is himself that he loses".

    Together with this we now take the second revision.   Pater gives a
translation from Victor Hugo, but the translations have a different
stress in the two versions:

        PWM. 212: "we have an interval and then we cease to be."

        R1 312 :   "We have an interval, and then our place knows us
                no more."

Did Pater when he prepared the constituents of THE RENAISSANCE for
publication think that the original passage was a little too sombre for
the imminent readers?   There may be a clear difference of meaning
between "then we cease to be" and "our place knows us no more," or,
though they could be read to mean the same thing - extinction - they
could equally well be read to mean two different ideas, the second

conforming to a religious belief that we have "passed on". It is
interesting to observe that Pater, at all times in his career, would
bend but not break: he would alter the wording of a sentence or
phrase so that it would assume an inoccuous form, but without really
renegading on his original meaning. This will be found to be true of
later revisions.

The "Conclusion" was omitted without explanation, from the second
edition of the book (renamed: THE RENAISSANCE: STUDIES IN ART AND
POETRY) published in 1877, though when he replaced it in the third
edition of 1888 he provided a footnote which read:

> "This brief 'Conclusion' was omitted in the second edition
> "of this book, as I conceived it might possibly mislead some of
> "those young men into whose hands it might fall. On the whole
> "I have thought it best to reprint it here, with some slight
> "changes which bring it closer to my original meaning. I have
> "dealt more fully in Marius the Epicurean with the thoughts
> "suggested by it."

We must acknowledge that Pater was excessively timid. The aesthetic
movement was hardly fortunate in its progeniter, this quiet, shy, gentle
and gentlemanly Oxford don. He was not in any manner the stuff of
which leaders are made. Many instances of this timidity could be
quoted, but two are given below which may not be well-known:

In 1937 Miss Irene Cooper Willis published Vernon Lee's Letters in
a privately printed edition of 50 copies. She was the literary
executor and close friend of Miss Violet Paget (Vernon Lee) and was
able to transmit some personal memories of Pater, in addition to the
numerous references in the letters. Here is one short extract taken
from a letter to her 'Dearest Mamma" written on Wednesday Aug. 2 from
'Casa Pater, Oxford':

> "A very simple, amiable man, avowedly afraid of almost
> "everything . . . I cannot say how friendly these people ⌊Pater
> "and his sisters⌋ are"

The next quotation is from Aspects of Wilde, by Vincent O'Sullivan
(Constable: 1936) p. 11:

> "Walter Pater, he ⌈Wilde⌉ thought, was far too sensitive to the
> "criticisms of people not fit to tie his shoes. Once at Oxford
> "he came on Pater brooding over an article which attempted to
> "turn into ridicule his essay on Charles Lamb. The article was
> "entitled: "Lamb - and Mint Sauce" and was written, according to
> "Wilde, by H.D. Trail, a writer of considerable repute.
> "Wilde was dumbfounded. He said his estimate of Pater as a man
> "altered from that moment. "Just imagine Pater ! I could not
> "conceive how one could be Pater and yet be susceptible to the
> "insults of the lowest form of journalism." In that is all the
> "difference between Pater and the vulgarizer of Pater. Wilde
> "was more than that, but he was that too. He always professed a
> "great admiration for Pater's books. For the man he seemed to
> "have the slightly contemptuous pity of one who lives in the
> "sight of the public,despises it, and dominates it easily, for
> "another who dreads the public and is morbidly sensitive to its
> "hostility."

Though many reviews of the first edition of THE RENAISSANCE were favourable or at worst tepid, it did receive several thunderbolts of Victorian wrath which, bearing in mind Pater's gentle nature as mentioned above, might be sufficient to account for the omission of "Conclusion" from the second,1877, edition.

A comparison of the 1st and 3rd edition printings of this essay (RI and R3) shows thirty-eight points of difference. Of these revisions, only five are of significance: the others, though of interest from a stylistic point of view, do not make any appreciable alteration to the content of the essay. They are:

R1. p. 210: "The Service of philosophy, and of religion and culture as well . . . "

R3. p. 249: "The service of philosophy, of speculative culture . . . "

R1. p. 212: "or some abstract morality"

R3. p. 251: "or some abstract theory"

R1. p. 211: "Theories, religious or philosophical ideas"

R3. p. 251: "Philosophical theories or ideas"

R1. p. 212: "political or religious enthusiasm, or the enthusiasm of humanity."

R3. p. 252: "The various forms of enthusiastic activity, disinterested or otherwise, which come naturally to many of us."

R1. p. 212: "The wisest in art and song."

R3. p. 252: "The wisest, at least among "the children of this world", in art and song."

The total effect of the revisions is clear: any offending allusion to religion was removed, indeed the word 'religion', which appears three times in the first edition, is absent entirely from the third. We might well imagine that some ghostly father had blue-pencilled the essay and that the points of censure had been accepted in order that the work might entire polite society. We remember again Pater's well-known timidity, his resolve 'never to offend', yet notice that no one ever induced him to express any real and unequivocal statement of change of belief. To direct questions on his belief he would give a polite answer. We should also bear in mind his distaste of guiding criticism or belief by abstract theory. In the first page of his first book he says of writers who seek for universal formula in art or poetry "such discussions help very little . . . "

We now come to the comparison between the third edition of 1888 and the fourth, the last to be published in Pater's lifetime, in 1893, the year before he died. There are seventeen points of difference. Few contain any serious movement of ideas, the majority are concerned with

polishing and refining expression only.   Only one can be said to be of
any significance:

     R3. p. 252: "the love of art for art's sake"

     R4. p. 253: "the love of art for its own sake."

"Art for art's sake" had at that time come to assume unpleasant and
disturbing tones.   By 1893 Pater was an oldish, tired man.   The BNC
graduate of whom I wrote earlier told me that though he visited him
frequently in 1893—1894, when he came to think of it, he never saw Pater
'stand up.'   "When I attended him in his rooms he was either lying down
or seated in a chair."   The revision mentioned above was the last timid
gesture of non-attachment. It is again typical, however, of some inner
stubborness of Pater's mind that he did not alter the real central
content of his thought and argument: he refashioned the words, but did
not really abandon the essential meaning.

b. Multi-form articles

3. Wordsworth

This essay, in its various guises, appeared on no less than seven
occasions; some of them are only verbatim copies, others show
differences of arrangement and revision.   The seven items, all from the
same root-stock, are:

<table>
<tr><td></td><td></td><td align="right">No. in
Section Ia</td></tr>
<tr><td>1.</td><td>"On Wordsworth".

    Fortnightly Review (April 1874)</td><td align="right">17</td></tr>
<tr><td>2.</td><td>A much revised and reduced version of
the above essay appeared as a review
of three books of Wordsworth's
poetry in:

    Athenaeum (26 January 1889)</td><td align="right">61</td></tr>
<tr><td>3.</td><td>A review of the same three books was
printed in the:

    Guardian (27 February 1889)</td><td align="right">62</td></tr>
<tr><td>4.</td><td>The Fortnightly Review essay (No. 1 above)
was thoroughly revised and, with two extra
paragraphs, appeared in the first edition of
APPRECIATIONS (15 November 1889) as
"Wordsworth"</td><td align="right">71</td></tr>
<tr><td>5.</td><td>The Guardian review (No. 3 above) was
reprinted verbatim in
ESSAYS FROM THE 'GUARDIAN' p.p. (1896)</td><td align="right">100</td></tr>
<tr><td>6.</td><td>The Athenaeum review (No. 2 above) was
reprinted verbatim in
UNCOLLECTED ESSAYS (USA: 1903)</td><td align="right">101</td></tr>
<tr><td>7.</td><td>The same Athenaeum review was reprinted
in
SKETCHES AND REVIEWS (USAP 1919)</td><td align="right">103</td></tr>
</table>

NOTE: The Athenaeum review (Nos. 2, 6, and 7 above) has
not been published in either of the collected
editions of Pater's works (Edition de Luxe 1900/1901
and the New Library Edition 1910).

A general comment is that the changes between earlier and later
versions do not denote any noteworthy change of thought or feeling: the
alterations being mainly in variety of literary expression.

Thus we may take Nos. 1 and 4 together for comparison as being the

most important of the seven.   The <u>APPRECIATIONS</u> essay was a longer
version that the earlier one, and two paragraphs were inserted which
did not appear in the <u>Fortnightly Review</u>.   The first comes on p. 44
after the paragraph ending "particular spots" of time", and reads:

> "It is to such a world, and to a world of congruousmeditation
> "thereon, that we see him retiring in his but lately published
> "poem of <u>The Recluse</u> — taking leave, without much count of
> "costs, of the world of business, of action and ambition, as
> "also of all that for the majority of mankind counts as
> "sensuous enjoyment. * "

Together with this paragraph a long footnote is given regarding the
recent (1888) publication of <u>The Recluse</u>.   Pater here seems to have
taken the easier path to update the original article rather than
deciding to rewrite it completely.

A second lengthy insertion in 4 is found on p. 48 where the thirteen
lines commencing "In this sense the leader of the 'Lake School', in
spite of an earnest preoccupation with man, . . . " to the finish of
"had too potent a material life of their own to serve greatly his
poetic purpose." are fresh material.

There are also a number of smaller alterations; polishing and
scrubbing at the earlier version.   Here are a few examples which will
show their general trend:

1. p. 457: "It has been remarked, again and again; it reveals
   itself in many forms."

4. p. 41: "It has been remarked as a fact in mental history
   again and again. It reveals itself in many forms; "

1. p. 457: "and it falls into broad, untroubled spaces."

4. p. 41: "and it falls into broad, untroubled, perhspa
   somewhat monotonous spaces."

1. p. 457: "Subtle and sharp as he is in the outling of
   visible imagery, he is most subtle and delicate of all
   in the noting of sounds."

4. p. 43: "Clear and delicate at once, as he is in the
   outlining of visible imagery, he is more clear and
   delicate still, and finely scrupulous, in the noting
   of sounds;"

1. p. 458: "It was like a 'survival' of that primitive
   condition . . . "

4. p. 46: "It was like a 'survival,' in the peculiar
   intellectual temperament of a man of letters at the
   end of the eighteenth century, of that primitive
   condition . . . "

1. p. 461: "far bolder and more wondering spirits"

4. p. 53: "far more venturesome, perhaps errant, spirits"

It seems on the whole that Pater revised by replacing the simple with the complex, and by hovering around his expression with what might be thought to be a form of mental diffidence but was truly an effort to achieve a more exact expression of his thought. This was done maybe to some extent of set purpose as a reading of the essay on style will suggest.

We now come to the two reviews, Nos. 2 and 3 above, which both were published in the early part of 1889. They were reviews of the three books: The Complete Poetical Works of Wordsworth, intro. John Morley; The Recluse; and Selections from Wordsworth by William Knight and others. Both reviews were drawn from the earlier Fortnightly Review article, sometimes to the extent of exact quotation, in others by a free rephrasing of material, combined with linking passages. They were much shorter in total than the No. 1 version.

A comparison of the two reviews is very interesting. They were written within a month of each other, and the reviews were of the same books (see last paragraph). Pater evidently decided not to offer identical reviews to each periodical, yet abstained from composing completely different articles. His solution was to take the Fortnightly Review article and from it compose two shorter ones, each differing to a sufficient degree so that they could not be said to be identical, yet each being shall we say cousin of the other. A few details are given below to show the extent of the divergencies and similarities.

This can be taken in two parts. First there are the numerous sentences in which the same thought has been slightly recast. For example, the entire first paragraph of each review is now given:

2. Athenaeum. p. 109
   "The appearance of Prof. Knight's judicious 'Selections' and of
   "Messrs. Macmillan's collected edition of his works in one
   "volume, with the first book of 'The Recluse,' now printed in its
   "entirety for the first time, and a sensible introductory essay
   "by Mr. John Morley, gives sufficient proof that general interest
   "in Wordsworth is on the increase. Nothing could be better —
   "nothing so well calculated as a careful study of Wordsworth to
   "correct the faults of our bustling age as regards both thought
   "and taste, and remind people, amid the vast contemporary
   "expansion of the means and accessories of life of the essential
   "value of life itself. It was none other than Mill himself, so
   "true a representative of the main tendencies of the spirit of
   "our day, who protested that when the battle which he and his
   "friends were waging had been won the world would 'need more than
   "ever those qualities which Wordsworth had kept alive and
   "nourished.' "

3. Guardian. p. 317.
   "The Appearance, so close to each other, of Professor Knight's
   "careful and elaborately annotated "Selections from William
   Wordsworth," of Messrs. Macmillan's collected edition of the
   "poet's works, with the first book of the "Recluse," now

"published for the first time, and an excellent introductory
"essay by Mr. John Morley, forms a welcome proof that the study
" of the most philosophic of English poets is increasing among
"us. Surely nothing could be better, hardly anything more
"directly fitted than a careful reading of Wordsworth, to
"counteract the faults and offences of our busy generation, in
"regard both to thought and taste, and to remind people, amid
"the enormous expansion, at the present time, of all that is
"material and mechanical in life, of the essential value, the
"permanent ends, of life itself."

   The _Guardian_ review differs generally from the _Athenaeum_ in being
more wordy, more florid, more carefully wrought. Indeed, apart from
the fact that it came second in time as regards publication, we might
think on a close comparison that the _Athenaeum_ essay was taken as a
draft from which a more satisfactory and final job of work ensued.
Thus, to take a few random examples, we have:

   Athenaeum: "As much as possible."

   Guardian: "So far as can be ascertained."

   Athenaeum: "which has its obvious uses"
   Guardian: "which has indisputable recommendations"

   Athenaeum: "worldly prosperity De Quincey reckoned it"
   Guardian: "Long ago De Quincey noted it as a strongly
                  "determinant fact in Wordsworth's literary career,
                  "pointing, at the same time, to his remarkable good
                  "luck also, on the material side of life."

   Apart from differing shapings of the same sentence or paragraph,
there are instances where matter is inserted in one article but not in
the other. These will be found mainly in extending the length of the
Guardian review, it being more extensive than the Athenaeum version, and
a short account is now given of these instances. The following
additional passage in the _Guardian_ was taken from the _Fortnightly Review_
with slight alteration of wording:

   "Coleridge and other English critics at the beginning of the
   "present century had a great deal to say concerning a
   "psychological distinction, of much importance (as it appeared
   "to them) between the _fancy_ and the _imagination._ Stripped of a
   "great deal of somewhat obscure metaphysical theory, this
   "distinction reduced itself to the certainly vital one, with
   "which all true criticism more or less directly has to do,
   "between the lower and higher degrees of intensity in the poet's
   "conception of his subject, and his concentration of himself upon
   "his work. It was Wordsworth who made most of this distinction,
   "assuming it as the basis for the final classification
   "(abandoned, as we said, in the new edition) of his poetical
   "writings."

   Another long insertion is found in the _Guardian_ with the following:

"The poem of 'Resolution and Independence' is a storehouse of
"such records; for its fulness of lovely imagery it may be
"compared to Keats's 'Saint Agnes' Eve' . . . in a particular
"folding of the hills."

Both versions conclude with the same paragraph, differing only in
slight turns of expression - 2. "fine passages" 3. "striking passages"
- except that in the Athenaeum we are given a quotation:

"Thickets full of songsters, and the voice
"Of lovely birds, an unexpected sound

"Made for itself and happy in itself,
"Perfect contentment, Unity entire."   (23 lines quoted)

Referring to 6. UNCOLLECTED ESSAYS and 7. SKETCHES AND REVIEWS it
remains to say that Thomas B. Mosher and Albert Mordell, the editors in
each book, chose to reprint the Athenaeum review, while ESSAYS FROM THE
GUARDIAN (No. 5) is, as the name states, from the periodical of the same
name.

175

b. Multi-form articles

4. Coleridge

There are four papers to be considered:

The relationship between these essays is not difficult to follow.
The Westminster Review article (A. Review above) may be regarded as the
quarry from which the structure of C. APPRECIATIONS and D. Mordell was
erected. It was a long, rather involved, and certainly learned article
and does credit not only to its author and the periodical in which it
appeared, but also to the periodical public which seemed to take such
matter in its stride.

Twenty-four years after he had published the periodical essay (A.)
Pater compiled a volume of essays for a book titled APPRECIATIONS: WITH
AN ESSAY ON STYLE (C.). He decided to include an essay on Coleridge and
to use the earlier article for this. One difficulty was that the
A. Review item considered Coleridge mainly in his position as a figure
of his age, and dealt with his philosophical approach to current
problems. The book APPRECIATIONS was intended to deal entirely with

literary topics and therefore it would not be sufficient to reproduce
the Coleridge essay from A. Review as it stood.   In addition to this,
Pater was not entirely happy with the essay as may be seen from a letter
he wrote to William Sharp, Nov. 4th, 1882 (see William Sharp: A Memoir
compiled by his wife: 1910, pp. 67-68 and LWP. No. 69):

> "The list you sent me is complete with the exception
> "of an article on Coleridge in the Westminster of January
> "1866, with much of which, both as to matter and manner,
> "I should now be greatly dissatisfied. The article is
> "concerned with S.T.C.'s prose; but, corrected, might
> "be put alongside of the criticism of his verse which I
> "made for Ward's 'English Poets'.

He therefore took the A. Review and scored out a good half of it,
mainly those portions that dealt with philosophical problems, leaving
the paragraphs which gave a view of Coleridge as a writer.   To
strengthen this he added to the essay the Introduction which he had
written in 1880 to a selection of Coleridge's works at the request of
his friend T. Humphrey Ward, editor of a four volume anthology
The English Poets.

    When in 1919 Albert Mordell, an American man of letters, decided to
publish a volume of uncollected writings of Pater, he included in his
book SKETCHES AND REVIEWS those portions of A. Review which Pater had
omitted from APPRECIATIONS and placed them under a title of his own
devising "Coleridge as a Theologian"

    A few words on those portions of A. Review which were used for
C. APPRECIATIONS.   In general we may note two tendencies in Peter's
adaptation.   He tried as far as possible to make the essay more easy to
read, having in mind no doubt a wider and more general type of reader.
Thus, the well read subscribers of the Westminster Review might not their
heads sagely at:

> "Such is the charm of Julian, perhaps of Luther; in the
> "narrow compass of modern times, of Dr. Newman and
> "Lacerdaire; it is also the peculiar charm of Coleridge . ."
> (p. 1o7)

but in APPRECIATIONS, this became:

> "Such has been the charm of many leaders of lost causes
> "in philosophy and in religion. It is the special charm
> "of Coleridge . . . "

Here and there passages are omitted from C. APPRECIATIONS with perhaps
the same motive:

> "A transcedentalism that makes what is abstract more
> "excellent than what is concrete has nothing akin to
> "the leading philosophies of the world."

Sometimes a long portion of A. Review has been reduced to a mere
linking sentence with no attempt to produce even a precis of the
original.   Thus the four pages 108-11 of A. Review "Coleridge failed
in that attempt . . . the eclaircissement of the eighteenth century" in
which Coleridge is compared with Wordsworth, what is a philosophical

idea of the former appearing as a sentiment or instinct in the latter —
is pared down to a mere summary sentence: "It was an effort, surely an
effort of sickly thought, that saddened his mind, and limited the
operation of his unique poetic gift." It does seem though that this
particular elision impairs the continuity of thought in APPRECIATIONS
because the next sentence in which both versions join forces again,
does notmake its point: "So what the reader of our generation will
least find in Coleridge's prose writings is the excitement of the
literary sense." I may remark here that, owing to Pater's habit of
dressing an article up in other clothes this happened with other items,
as he was well aware. In a letter concerning another essay, on "Bruno"
he writes: "The article is really a chapter from an unfinished work,
and had to be cut about for insertion in the Review. This may have
given it an inexplicable air here and there".

Further, readers of APPRECIATIONS were not expected to plough their
way through long quotations, and a number of these were omitted from the
book though they were printed in the Review.

A number of purely biographical details of interest to literary
students were not transcribed for the book, their omission being most
skilfully arranged.

These were all matters of literary taste and discretion, but there
is one other type of alteration/omission which is of a different order.
The Westminster Review reader was probably well aware of the main events
of Coleridge's life, and of his weaknesses and lapses. Pater saw no
point in parading these failings before the world, and omitted from
APPRECIATIONS a number of references to Coleridge's drug taking habits,
and the effects they had on his work.

The SKETCHES AND REVIEWS editor was not without his own difficulties
He took it that APPRECIATIONS omitted consideration of Coleridge as a
theologian, and named his extract, for so it is, accordingly. In his
determination to render to art what belonged to art, and to theology
the theology of the Review, he had to make some peculiar effects. P.117
Review reads: " . . . to the questions oftheology and art-criticism."
Pater revised this for APPRECIATIONS as "to the questions of theology,
and poetic or artistic criticism", while SKETCHES AND REVIEWS must
needs cheat with " . . . to the question of theology" with a firm full
stop and then, as we are to read of works of art, place four dots in a
line
       . . . .
and back out for seven pages.

Apart from these linking alterations, Mordell transcribed
faithfully those portions of A. Review which were not found in
APPRECIATIONS, the declared intention being to publish work by Pater
which is not to be found in his published books.

APPENDICES

c.   WALTER H. PATER

1.   Pater as a Lecturer

The following books and periodicals contain references to Pater as a lecturer:

Bathe, Rev. Anthony
see T. Wright, The Life of Walter Pater (1907), pp. 236, 239

Bathe was a pupil of Pater and in a letter to Wright describes Pater's early Brasenose College lectures, particularly one on Virgil's Georgics

Benson, A.C.
Walter Pater (English Men of Letters series)
Macmillan and Co. Limited; 1906

There is nothing original here, the details being taken from other writers

Birchall, Rev. Oswald
see T. Wright, The Life of Walter Pater (1907), p. 239

Birchall was another pupil of Pater and gives an interesting account of Pater lecturing on Aristotle.

Ward, T. Humphrey
Brasenose College Quatercentenary Monographs 2 vols. in 3
Vol. II (III) Mon. XIV. 2c. "Brasenose 1864-1872". pp. 74,75,77

This monograph deals with Pater's early lectures.
"A few of us found in these lectures an extraordinary stimulous"

Farnell, Lewis R.
An Oxonian Looks Back
Martin Hopkinson Ltd.: 1934

This is the autobiography of an Oxford man: Fellow of Exeter College; Vice-Chancellor of the University. He travelled extensively but the core of his world was Oxford.

Contains a few references to Pater and his sister Clara. There is a particularly interesting description of Pater as a lecturer on archaic Greek Art. He makes the claim for Pater as an innovator in Greek studies "though his sensitive and retiring nature would have shrunk from being called the father of anything."

Evans, Lawrence
    Letters of Walter Pater
        Oxford at the University Press: 1970

    pp. 5 and n., 21n., 114 & n., 115 & n., 116 & n., 128 & n.

    Useful facts concerning Pater's first lectures and later
    individual lectures.

[Field, Michael]
Works and Days: from the Journal of Michael Field
edited by T. & D.C. Sturge Moore
    John Murray: 1933

pp. 118, 121, 122

    An interesting description of Pater's lecture on Prosper
    Mérimée at the London Institution, Finsbury Circus, London,
    24th November, 1890, and one on Wordsworth the day before, 23rd
    November at Toynbee Hall.

MacColl, D.S.
    "A Batch of Memories XII. Walter Pater"
        The Week-end Review.
            IV. No. 92 (12 November 1931), 759-760

Very interesting details of Pater's appearance and manner from an
undergraduate who attended Pater in his rooms for lectures on
Plato's Republic.

Titchener, E.B.
    "Walter Horatio Pater", Book Reviews
        New York: Macmillan and Co.: October 1894, pp. 201-205

This was an obituary notice by an undergrauate admirer and contains
very interesting first-hand accounts and reminiscences of Pater,
his appearance, rooms at Brasenose College, manner, together with a
number of amusing anecdotes.

There is an account of Pater lecturing on Plato and Platonism in
his rooms to a group of students.   As this periodical is not easy
to come by, an extract is given below:

    "We sat where there were sitting-places; at the table, in
    "arm-chairs, on the window-seat.   Pater liked to be listened
    "to, and did not like to have his every word noted down. But
    "there were one or two of us who had equal objection to letting
    "his words escape us. We hit upon a compromise. Some few of
    "us would listen, writing nothing, and endeavour to hold the
    "lecturer's eye; the others wrote for dear life, and forewent
    "the understanding of what they heard till the hour was over.
    "Of course the ruse was seen through, as many an amused smile
    "showed, but no rebuke came.

        "The little heap of paper slips was never absent from the
    "lecturer's table.   On each one of these was written some one

"thought, phrases expressing some particular aspect or part-
"aspect of the subject in hand. This was Pater's way, and
"he more than once recommended it to us as the preliminary to
"essay-writing. Some one thing that struck us as worth the
"saying was to be put, as well as we could put it, on its
"special slip; and other things in like manner upon others.
"Then the papers were to be shuffled this way and that, like
"a paper of cards, and the final arrangement of their ideas
"only decided on after long testing and re-testing. Oftentimes
"he said this mere machanical juxtaposition of thought with
"thought gave one new thoughts; and in any case the first
"order of writing was not to be trusted as the best order of
"expounding. I believe that this was the method followed by
"him in his own published writings. At least he always
"favored it in conversation; and I have heard an unfriendly
"critic say that he could 'see the joins' in the Marius"

Wright, Thomas
    The Life of Walter Pater
        Everett & Company: 1907

    Vol. I. pp. 236, 239

        II   47 - 48

    Wright's sources of information are sometimes suspect

_____

Oxford University Gazette

    Lists of the combined University lectures
    were published from 1873 onwards.

    Pater's name features regularly from 1873 to 1891.

1867   Pater commenced lecturing at Brasenose
                        College, Oxford "in the spring of 1867"
                        LWP. No. 8 & n.

                        "about May 1867 came his first lectures
                        . . . 'The History of Philosophy' "
                        T. Humphrey Ward, quoted by A.C. Benson,
                        Walter Pater (1906) p. 20.

                        Lectures in the Georgics
                        "Divinity Lectures"
                        see T. Wright, Life of Walter Pater (1907)
                        pp. 236, 239

1871 — 1891   Combined University Lectures
                        Plato. The Republic
                        Aristotle. Ethics
                        Oxford University Gazette.

1873 Easter term   "History of Greek Philosophy"
                        University combined lecture.

1875 Hilary term   "Philosophical Questions"
                        University combined lecture

1875. 29 Nov.   "The Myth of Demeter and Persephone"   20
                        Birmingham & Midland Institute
                        (see also Section Ic: Location of
                         published manuscripts)
                        Printed in the Fortnightly Review
                        1 Jan. & 1 Feb. 1876

1878 13 April   "On 'Love's Labours Lost' "   26
                        Paper read before the New Shakespeare
                        Society.
                        Printed in Macmillan's Magazine Dec. 1885

1878 Michaelmas   "History of Greek Art with Books I,
     term   V. and VI of Pausanias"
                        University combined lecture
                        Draft manuscript of 'The Marbles of Aegina'
                        at Harvard University

                        "The Beginnings of Greek Sculpture"
                        Fortnightly Review . 1 Feb. & 1 Mar. 1880   30

                        "The Marbles of Aegina"
                        Fortnightly Review. 1 April 1880   31
                        "The Age of Athletic Prizemen"   89
                        Contemporary Review. Feb. 1894

                    Published in book form (posthumous):
                    GREEK STUDIES: A SERIES OF ESSAYS (1895)   97

1880 ?   "Humanism"
                    South Place Chapel, Finsbury
                    Toynbee Hall, Whitechapel.
                    see T. Wright, Life of Walter Pater (1907)
                    pp. 47-48, Vol. II.
                    (Wright's source for this information is
                    suspect).

1890 17 Nov.   "Prosper Merimee"   78
                    Taylor Institute, Oxford
       24 Nov.   London Institution
                    Printed in the Fortnightly Review
                    December 1890
                    see LWP. No. 190
                        Michael Field. Works and Days (1933)
                        pp. 119-121

1890 23 Nov.   "Wordsworth"
                    Toynbee Hall, Whitechapel.
                    see LWP. 191 & n.
                    (Toynbee Hall - a social settlement in
                    Whitechapel, erected in memory of the
                    social reformer, Arnold Toynbee (1852
                    -1883) who had been a contemporary of
                    Oscar Wilde at Oxford . Rupert Hart-Davis)

1891 Hilary Term   "Plato and Platonism"
                    University combined lectures
                    Three lectures printed in periodicals:
                    "The Genius of Plato"
                        Contemporary Review (Feb. 1892)   80
                    "A Chapter on Plato" renamed in the
                    book as "Plato and the Doctrine of
                    Motion"
                        Macmillan's Magazine (May 1892)   81
                    "Lacedaemon"
                        Contemporary Review (June 1892)   82

                    Printed in book form:
                    PLATO AND PLATONISM: A SERIES OF LECTURES   87
                    (1893)

1892 2 August   "Leonardo da Vinci"
                    Delegates for the Extension of Teaching
                    beyond the limits of the University of
                    Oxford. (and Toynbee Hall ?)

APPENDICES

C.   WALTER H. PATER

Introduction to AN ENGLISH POET

The Fortnightly Review
1 April 1931. CXXIX n.s. , 433-435

When Mr. Pater died in 1894, there was found among his papers a
certain amount of fragmentary work, including a few incomplete chapters
of Gaston de Latour, what promised to be a characteristically penetrating
study of Dr. Johnson, and an essay entitled Imaginary Portraits 2. An
English Poet. All these were written in his own exquisite handwriting
in the manner peculiar to him, on quarto-size white or bluish-tinted
paper with carefully spaced lines, the blanks left here and there to be
filled in, after laborious thought and search, with two, sometimes three,
possible words, from which, in the end, "le mot juste" was to be chosen;
the closely-packed leaves, each one numbered, and so, page after page,
finished at last, and tied together finally with a neat scrap of ribbon.
From this meticulously careful and uniform method, Mr. Pater never seems
to have deviated. It is a witness to the spirit of the artist to whom
fidelity in detail meant what it means to the architect, or to the
builder of a great ship; an inalienable and essential part of the
perfected work. Those who knew Mr. Pater personally, or those who
seem to see the reflection of his elusive, austere, high-souled
character in what he wrote and the way in which he wrote, must needs be
struck by the singular quality of the style and the man - the subtle
blending of strength and beauty, of power and delicacy, of restraint and
imagination, of the Puritan and the Platonist - which gives him an
individual stamp and an individual place among great English prose
writers. "He who blows through brass may breath through silver."

The title of the essay printed here is significant - Imaginary
Portrait Number 2. The first essay to be published under a similar
heading was that most perfect autobiographical gem, The Child in the
House, which appeared in Macmillan's Magazine in August 1878. Closely
associated with this is Emerald Uthwart, the sober and moving record of
those far-off, unforgettable days and experiences of the writer's

boyhood under the shadow of the Cathedral at Canterbury. It was
written soon after Mr. Pater's visit to his old school, in the summer of
1891, a visit which revived fading memories and evoked an eager response
to the impressions of the moment. "The very place one is in, its
stone-work, its empty places, invade you, invade all who belong to them
as Uthwart belongs, yielding wholly from the first." Or later on, in
allusion to the second character-building environment of his early life:
"In truth, the memory of Oxford made almost everything he saw after it
seem vulgar." Again - and indeed a short sentence seems to reveal the
very heart of the essay "the mere beauties of the place counted at the

moment for less than in retrospect." Emerald Uthwart was published in
1892, in two consecutive numbers of the New Review. In his collected
works both of these essays are included in the volume entitled
Miscellaneous Studies. Of the three Mr. Pater himself gave the name
Imaginary Portrait only to the Child in the House and to the hitherto
unpublished English Poet, as if these two contained some deeper, more
intimate self-revelation than Emerald Uthwart even. And, in all three,
as in the final script of the Prelude, the reader discerns the "finer
sort of memory, bringing its object to mind with great clearness, yet,
as sometimes happens in dreams, raised a little above itself and above
ordinary retrospect."

Autobiography of such sort may lack what is commonly called veracity
but it has the added quality, an aroma of the past. It is indeed "of
quality and fabric divine."

After Mr. Pater's death, Dr. Shadwell and Sir Herbert Warren
examined the few stray MSS, and rejected for publication, on the ground
of their incompleteness, the unfinished chapters of Gaston, and, one
imagines, the essay on Dr. Johnson and An English Poet. It is true
that a certain part of the unfinished Gaston was selected by them, and
incorporated in the book as the reader knows it, but it was felt at the
moment that all other fragmentary or incompleted work should be left
unpublished. But, as time passed, it became more and more clearly
evident that this delicate flexible prose was to find a lofty and
permanent place in English Literature. In the light of this fact it
would seem an ill-judged surrender to conditions and opinions of thirty
years standing, to withold from publication this early attempt to define,
and reveal the growth of those qualities which the reader of Mr. Pater
associates with all his work. That it is the study of a young
aspiring artist lends to its interest. Posterity eagerly seized upon
the immature or fragmentary works of poets and of painters and has found
even, as e.g. in Leonardo's study of St. Anne, a deeper significance and
a deeper satisfaction than in his more finished work. The 'faultless
painter' struck and still strikes, the authentic note:

> "Their works drop groundward, but themselves, I know
> Reach many a time a heaven that's shut to me;
> Enter, and take their place there sure enough,
> Though they came back and cannot tell the world."

In this early essay, with its intimate self-revelation, the
sympathetic reader is privileged to discern the latent characteristics
which moulded Mr. Pater's unique style, a style so wholly personal and
inimitable, style so closely often to poetry, yet in its
intelectuallity, its reserve, its strength, exalted into such noble
and spendid prose. The idea, running like a thread of gold through
the whole essay — the blendid imagery of the honeysuckle in its frail
and fleeting beauty of colour and scent, with the delicate power of the
flower metal-screen work, haunting the growing boy like a passion, never
to leave him in all his later years — how symbolic of the character and
the work of the writer ! All the superficial, stupid, cruel and crude
misjudgments of those early years crumble into dust in the face of the

185

halting sincerity of a young man, trying to reveal himself to himself,
in this most intimate attempt.

"Afterwards when he was understood to be a post, this, a peculiar
character as of flowers in metal, was noticed by the curious as a
distinction in verse, such an elastic force in word and phrase,
following a delicate thought or feeling, as the metal followed the
curvature of the flower, or seemed to indicate an artistic triumph
over a material partly resisting, which yet at last took outline from
his thought with the firmness of antique forms of mastery."

The editor of this essay has touched it as little as is possible.
Of a choice of words, that written last, or at top of one or two others,
is as a rule, printed here; defective words or phrases are marked by
brackets or a question mark. Sometimes, in the original essay, the
grammar is faulty, and therefore the sense is obscure. The editor
has taken the liberty of cutting out one or two unessential passages.
What is left would seem to be "of a quality and fabric" such as no
lover of Walter Pater would willingly let die." [M.O.]

It has seemed worth while to print this introduction for the

light it throws on the manuscripts left by Walter Pater and for the

paper it preceded.

The editor was Mrs May Ottley, a pupil of Clara Pater when the

latter was tutor and Vice-Principal of Summerville College, Oxford.

Later, the two women became close friends. Mrs Ottley and her

husband, Cannon Robert Lawrence Ottley, were the good angels of the

Pater sisters: Clara Ann and Hester Maria.

I am indebted to the holder of the copyright and the editor of
the Contemporary Review for joint permission to reprint this item.

C.   WALTER H. PATER

                  3. Sermon preached in Brasenose Chapel
                     October 1894. (Luke XI. 52)

                     Rev. Dr. F.W. Bussell

     We have lately lost a pattern of the student life, an example of the
mind which feels its own responsibilities, which holds and will use the
key of knowledge; severely critical of itself and its performances; and
an indulgent censor; a sympathetic adviser. At an age when some men
begin to turn in to themselves, and lose sympathy with younger ones and
the rapid generations of undergraduate life, he maintained an unflagging
interest in the doings of the college, in the essays ofthe men, in those
unique lectures, prepared with such care and delivered with such modesty
It was not his way to compel the idle; he recognised that the newly-
enfranchised must be left to the responsibility of choice;he preferred
to be sought by those who were willing to take the trouble.   I do not
think that anyone who did so can help looking back to that first making
his acquaintance as an important moment in his university career; or
that anyone will forget the kind way in which he tried to discover the
signs of merit before he ventured to disapprove.   He was a model of
forbearance; and I well remember on one occasion his indignation with
himself and self-reproach because he had allowed his tongue to speak
with unfamiliar severity of some one absent, and who, I believe,
deserved it.

     Naturally inclined to a certain rigour in discipline, he was full of
excuse for individial cases; and regretted, and thought over stern
measures more than most members of a governing body can afford to do.
The pains he took about his frequent hospitality was a sign of the
conscientious thoroughness with which he performed the most trivial
actions of life.   And this explains the slowness of his composition;
and the classical smallness of the bulk of his writing.

     To a certain extent, but to a certain extent only, these may be
taken as an index to his character, as unveiling the true man.   But to
those who knew him as he lived here they seemed a sort of disguise.
There was the same tenderness, the same tranquillizing repose about his
conversation that we find in his writings; the same carefulness in
trifles, and exactness of expression.   But his written works betray
little trace of that child-like simplicity, that naive joyousness, that
never wearying pleasure in animals and their ways, that grave and yet
half-amused seriousness in which he met the events of the daily routine.
His habits were precise and austere, in some respects simple to the last

degree; as unlike the current and erroneous impression which certain
passages of his books may leave as it is possible to conceive. Almost
the sole luxury that he allowed himself was a bowl of rose-leaves,
preserved by an old lady in the country from a special recipe, and sent
every year as a present to him and a reminder of her friendship.   He
did not accumulate around him an increasing number of necessary props
of life, as so many men of sedentary life are unhappily tempted to do.
He never smoked; rarely took tonic, or medicine of any kind; and he
has left an example which it would be well if some student would follow;
spending his morning in writing or lecturing, some part of the afternoon
in correcting the composition of noon, and in the evening closing his
books completely; regarding it as folly to make for idleness in the
day by unseasonable labour at a time when reading men are best in bed.

     In consequence of this ascetic and simple life, he was never
depressed; he was absolutely and always the same.   There was only one
point in which he wished the sterner regimen could be revived; namely,
that Sunday morning chapel should be made compulsory.   Always regular
there himself, he felt real pain at the scanty attendance, and used to
trouble himself a great deal when some of his pupils abandoned the idea
of taking Holy Orders after coming up with that career in prospect. The
entire interest of his later years was religious; not, as some would
put it, ecclesiastical, though he was keenly sensible of their influence of
stately ritual, and to the last was planning schemes of a decoration of
our East End, a hope of beautifying which was very near to his heart.
In the Chapel service he took great delight, sometimes regretting that
the ardour of singing you showed in the Psalms seemed to abate when you
came to the Magnificat, which was to him above all others the song of
songs.   Another alteration he would have liked was the introduction of
music into our monthly mid-day celebration, from which he was never
absent when resident in college.

     Many of you will doubtless have read in one notice, how to a young
student he once confessed that now he read little else but the Bible,
the Prayer Book, and the Breviary.   It is quite true that his interests,
as the years passed over him, centred more and more on the Liturgy and
fabrics of the Catholic church; on the truths of the creed from a High
Church standard and on the education of the young in the faith of their
fathers. He omce said that he had often wished to become a clergyman.
He was never happier than when discussing some of the cardinal
mysteries of the faith; and I well recall how he would reprove any
sympton of a rationalising spirit.

     This picture of the student of deep religious feeling, of
transparent naturalness, or ready humour, of unfailing courtesy, of
simple life, of austere and uniform diet (except when he entertained) -
this is a very different picture from that which some men have formed of
him, judging from stray passages here and there in his writings.   But
this is the way in which he would wish to be represented in his own
chapel to those who remember him, and before those, to whom, alas! he
must be but a name.

     (A later addition:)

188

I am glad of the opportunity of adding a few more words; words that I could not have uttered on the former occasion. Many will be disappointed at the meagreness of the reminiscence, or the coldness of the language. But they will, I feel sure, pardon me for the restraint which I have put upon my pen, knowing that tongue and voice would have failed me had I attempted to publish my real feelings. In such a place too, purely personal memories of an almost constant companion would have been inopportune unless they had conveyed some lesson. And surely it was not wrong to confine myself to just those secrets of his inner life, about which there are abroad, perhaps, some false impressions, even among those who fancied they knew him best. The genuiness of his piety, the simplicity, cheerfulness, and unselfishness of his daily life, his extraordinary and unusual care for the feelings (or the comforts) of others, - these are the things that I remember best about him; these are too the points on which but few are qualified to speak. Others will write with a finer appreciation of the unique style and beauty of his literary works; which, apart from their intrinsic art in thought or arrangement, had a strange soothing and elevating effect even upon those who could but imperfectly understand the language or the allusions.

But it was my peculiar privilege (the loss of which I have scarcely yet realised) to meet him, daily and hourly, rather as a man than as a writer; and so to listen to his ordinary talk, not upon art, (I should have been but an inept scholar and listener), but upon religion, chapel services, sermons, undergraduates, books, essays, cats, entertainments, and the attraction of nature, which we noticed on our frequent walks into the country, of which he was passionately fond. It was the happiest blanding of seriousness and mirth, of deep feeling and a sort of child-like glee in the varying surfaces of things. His whole life seemed to me to be the gradual consecration of an exquisite sense of beauty to the highest ends; an almost literally exact advance through the stages of admiration in the Symposium, till at last he reached the sure haven, the one Source of all that is fair and good. Not without significance, Pascal was the last character he undertook to portray (as only he could !) in a public lecture.

It is not here or now that I should write about his domestic affections, the break in which is almost the only sad thing about his sudden departure hence. We do not say as of old [Greek quotation] but I think we look to home life as to an unerring testimony to a man's true character. Nor again can I say much about my own private loss, which I have only just begun to feel, and shall feel more and more keenly daily and hourly.

It seems strange to us, in these days of rapid disillusionment within college life, that a man of his fastidious tastes should have contentedly born for eight and twenty years this luxious discomfort, this continuous residence in a society often exuberant and boisterous is spirits. But it never seemed for a moment to occur to him as possible to carry out the ideal or the practical side of college life, without living within constant call of his pupils. All those (who took the trouble to avail themselves of this wonderful chance) will remember his easy accessibility (for in spite of the many interruptions

he suffered I never once saw his 'oak' shut), his ready sympathy and
pretended leisure, - for it was the extreme of his politeness to
always appear to the visiter as having nothing to do; and his
invariable change of seat from fire to window, that the caller might
have the benefit of the only easy chair. We miss such a man in a
hundred little ways; at every turn some remembrance of his kindness
or his mirth rises up unbidden; his daily habits (we can say that of
but few nowadays) were woven inextricably into the texture of public
life.

     His death took place on the very day for which he had planned a
visit to an old farmhouse of mine in Devon; with infinite forethought
and care mapped out for the pleasure of his sisters, and by me
expected with keen anticipation of walks and drives together. I well
recall the zest with which he entered into the projected excursion,
the minuteness of every detail considered, and the too generous
payment to my tenant which he stipulated to be allowed to make. I
have left the original remarks exactly as they were delivered, and add
these few and digressive words partly to justify my choice of memories
here, partly to show how greatly in a college is felt the rare death of
a resident without whom it seems impossible to conceive the society or
the daily routine. I have purposely omitted all references to merits
known to a very wide circle, and thought of him (as he would wish to
be remembered) as an affectionate friend, a loyal and interested
college teacher, a devout Christian.

                                        F.W. Bussell